Seamless Embroidery

42 Projects and Patterns to Explore the Magic of Repeating Designs

YUMIKO HIGUCHI

ROOST BOOKS

Flower Row / Full-sized insert, Side B

An unbroken line of botanical flowers.

Contents

Note: Any and all of the projects included in this book are prohibited from commercial use or sale. Please enjoy handcrafting them for your own purposes.

Introduction

This book is a collection of connected embroidery patterns.

Embroidery uses a needle and thread to express connection. It's a comforting art form that with each and every connected stitch evokes thoughts and pleasures and cultivates a relaxing time. I'm aware of this whenever I do embroidery.

Whether it's beloved family and friends, day-to-day life, weekend plans, an upcoming travel itinerary, cityscapes, lush forests, or clouds against the sky, my mind is filled with all sorts of delightful things, and I'm able to create a variety of connecting patterns in which the needle is in dialogue with the thread and the fabric.

Through this book I feel even more connected with all of you out in the world, and it's my hope that together we can all create the pattern of a future that stretches out before us with seamless happiness.

—YUMIKO HIGUCHI

CLOCK
page 79

The hands tick off a light rhythm on
the embroidered face of this clock.

KITCHEN MITT

page 80

Even just as decoration, the design of this
kitchen mitt will brighten up the kitchen.
This is a right-handed mitt, but the pattern
and instructions can be reversed.

Chatty Girls | page 62

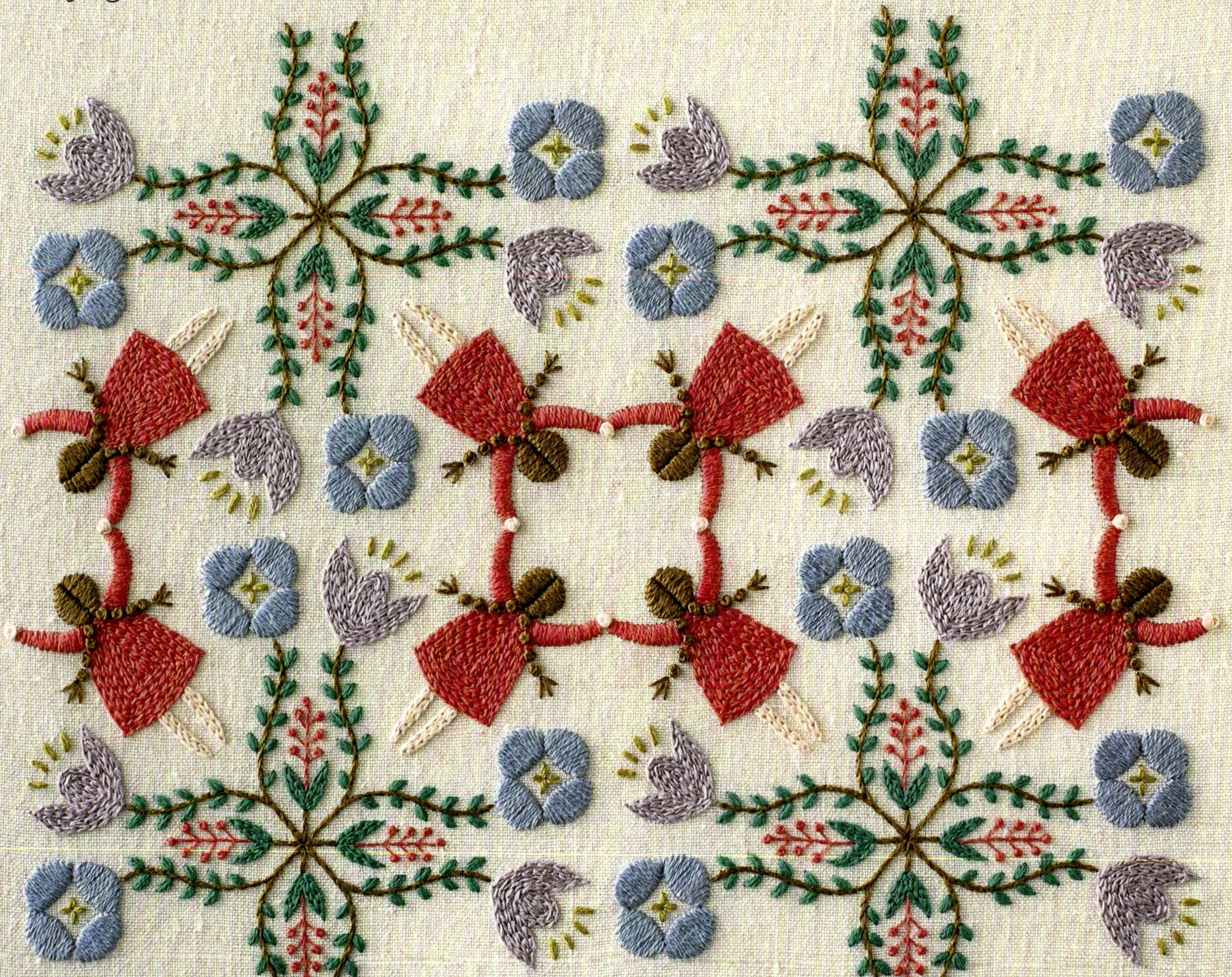

SANITARY CASE

page 81

I designed this with the idea that it
would make a lovely present for a girl.

GIFT BAG
page 82

Tie a ribbon around this gift bag that is already embellished with lots of ribbons. Be bold—make it in a chic color combination.

OBLONG POUCH

page 83

The carousel horses are aligned on the
flap of this splendidly embroidered pouch.
Let it bring back a memorable time.

PLANTER COVER

page 84

The embroidery goes all the way around, so this planter cover is darling from any angle. It has a loop so that it can also be hung as decoration.

COASTER

page 85

This polygonal design builds upon the
hexagonal nature of the pattern.
A subtle motif with an outsize impact.

HANGER COVER

page 86

Such a special hanger cover makes
opening your closet even more fun.

MINI POCHETTE

page 88

A small pochette features this repeating design delicately worked in a single-stranded pattern.

MINI CUSHION

page 89

This pattern brings to mind undulating waves and flowers strewn across the sea. It makes a beautiful addition to your interior decor.

KEY CASE
page 90

Choose your favorite houses as a motif. You can add a keyring on the inside to attach your keys.

BOOK COVER AND BOOKMARK

page 91

This pattern features a boulevard of autumn trees. The cover is the perfect size for a paperback, though you can adjust the dimensions to fit different book sizes.

CROWN

page 92

A soft linen crown elaborately embellished with a botanical pattern. It ties in the back with a ribbon.

DETACHED COLLAR
page 92

Pretty florets are scattered cleanly over this detached collar. The pattern is sized for an adult.

SHOULDER BAG

page 93

This arrangement uses just the outlines of the pattern in a single color. It makes the roses bloom all the more graphically.

DRAWSTRING PURSE

page 94

The scalloped bottom edge echoes the design.
The pattern is just as adorable upside down.

CLOTH BOX

page 95

Even the sides of this petite embroidered box are
covered with stitches. What will you put inside?

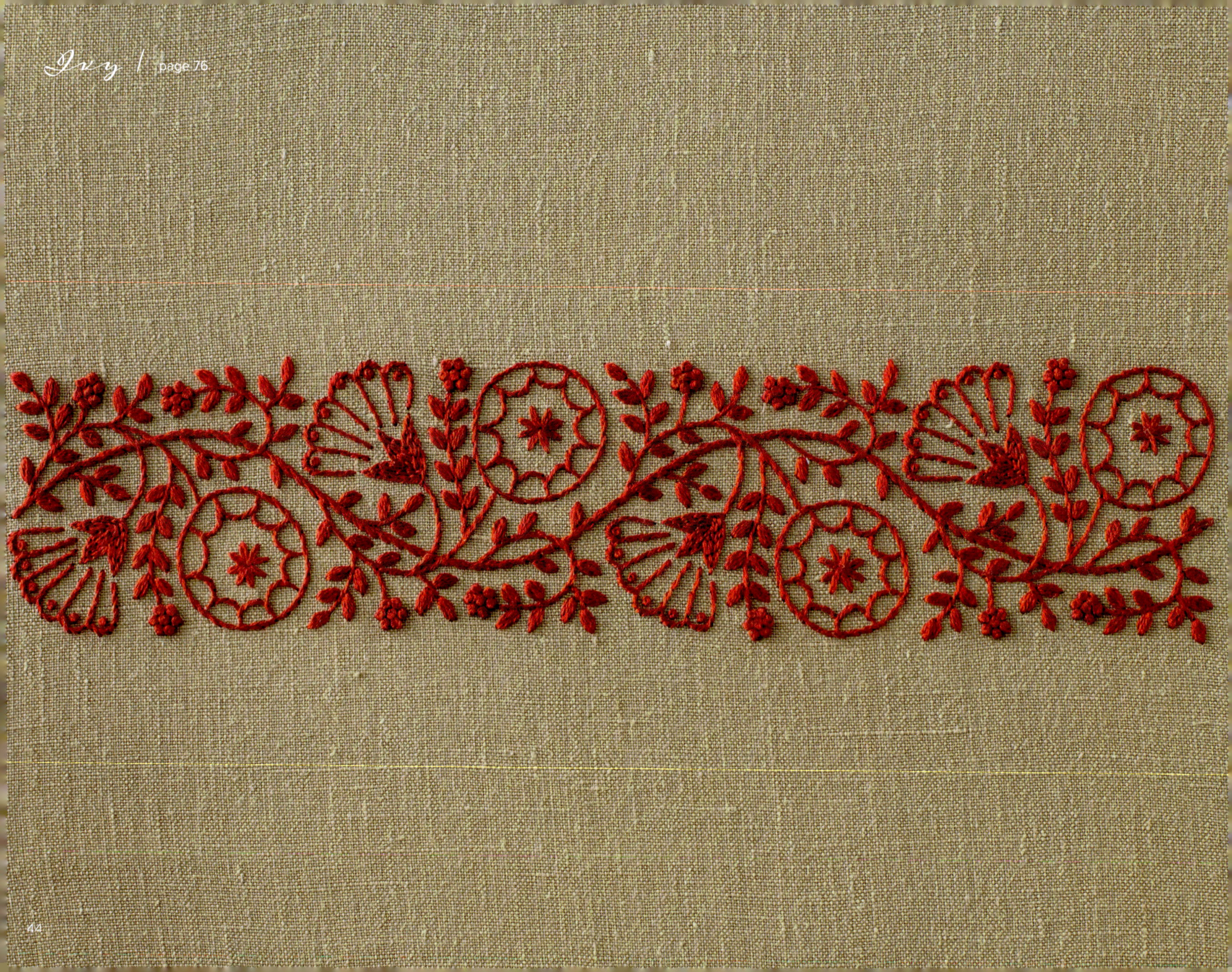

BRACELET
page 96

This soft cloth bracelet is gentle on the skin no matter how long you wear it.

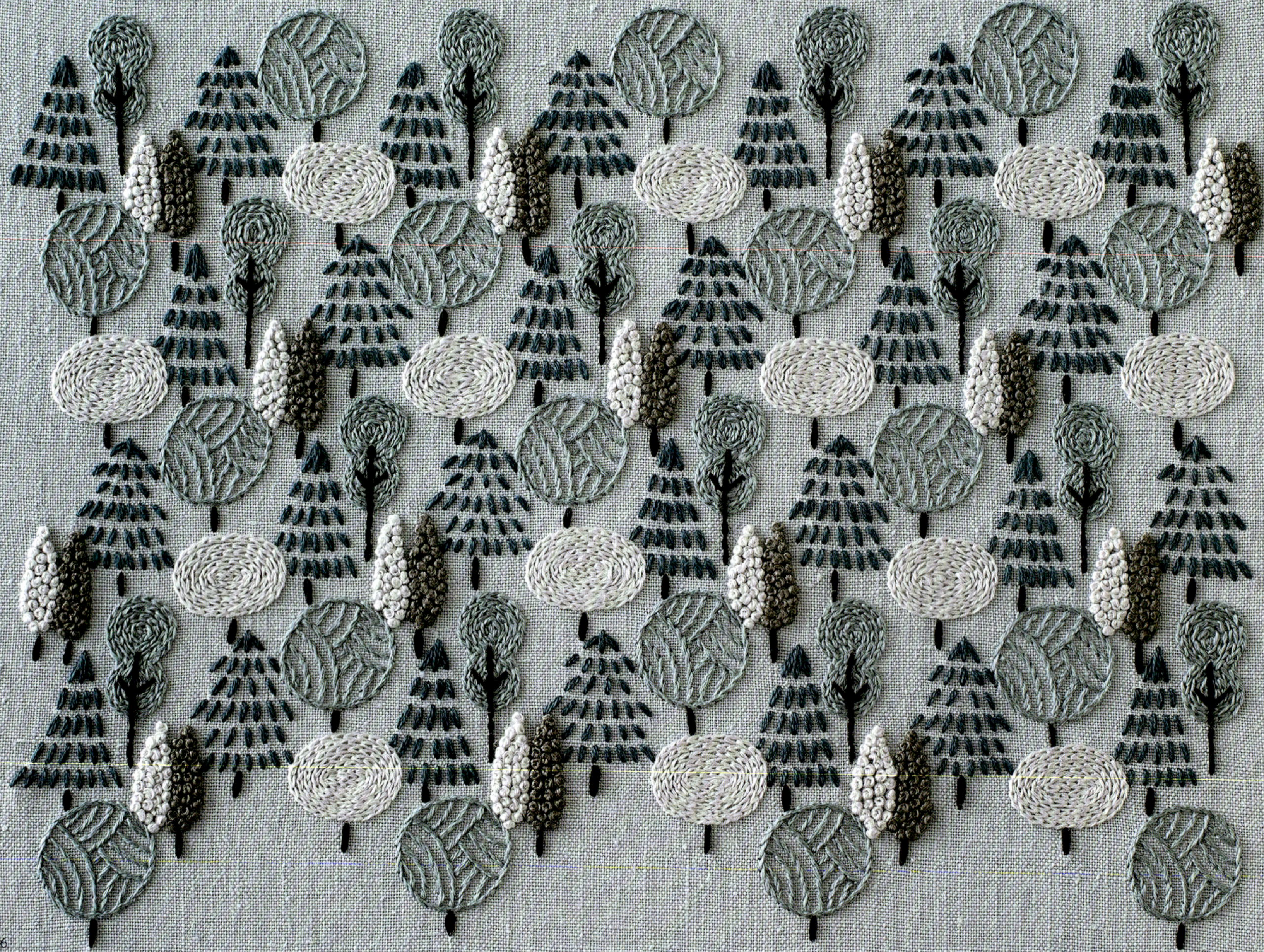

MOUNTAIN-SHAPED TEA COZY

page 97

This adorable tea cozy is like a little mountain for your tabletop! It's big enough to fit even a large teapot.

MINI BASKET

page 98

Which comes first, the chicken or the egg . . . ?
Just looking at this finished project is delightful.

A **Cellophane**
   Use this material to transfer patterns onto fabric so that the tracing paper doesn't tear.

B **Tracing Paper**
   This thin paper is for copying patterns.

C **Chalk Paper**
   Use this paper to transfer patterns onto fabric. For dark fabric, use white chalk paper.

D **Tailor's Shears**
   It's best to have sharp shears that are specifically made for cutting fabric.

E **Embroidery Scissors**
   Small, sharp, pointed scissors with a thin edge are the easiest to use.

F **Tracer**
   Use this tool to trace patterns when transferring onto fabric. You can also use a ballpoint pen.

G **Eyeleteer**
   Use this tool for perforations.

H **Needle Threader**
   This tool makes it easier to put the thread into the eye of a needle.

I **Needles and Pin Cushion**
   I use French embroidery needles with sharp points. The needle size depends on how many strands of embroidery floss are used.

J **Embroidery Hoops**
   Use embroidery hoops to stretch fabric tightly. I recommend the smaller 4" hoop, since it's a comfortable size to hold and work with when stitching. When working with a larger pattern, you may need to slide the hoop over your work. When stretching the fabric in your embroidery hoop, fasten the bracket securely. If your embroidery hoop is fastened too loosely, the fabric can sag and wrinkle. You can also wrap the inner hoop with bias tape or fabric (I recommend using white) to help prevent slippage.

EMBROIDERY FLOSS

For all the projects in this book, I used No. 25 embroidery floss. Six-stranded floss is the most popular. The brand I use is DMC embroidery floss from France, which is known for its vivid colors and lustrous texture.

FABRIC

All of the projects here are made using linen. Plain-weave linen is easy to work with, can be washed, and has a smooth texture, so it's perfectly suited for embroidery fabric. It's best to wash linen before cutting it to size, then dry it away from direct sunlight. To readjust the fabric grain, iron the linen lightly before it's completely dry. For *zakka* (small) projects, such as the kitchen mitt, quilt cloth is also used to provide a cushioned lining.

QUILT BATTING

When I want my zakka projects to be thick and fluffy, I use one-sided fusible quilt batting as padding. Use an iron to activate the adhesive on the reverse side of the fabric.

NUMBER OF STRANDS AND NEEDLE SIZE

Choose the size of your needle based on the number of strands you are using. By doing so, you'll always have the perfect needle for whatever project you're working on. The thickness of the fabric you're using also determines the size.

No. 25 Embroidery Floss	Embroidery Needle
6 strands	No. 3/4
3–4 strands	No. 5/6
1–2 strands	Nos. 7–10

*These are standard sizes of Clover needles.

Basic Stitches and Embroidery Fundamentals

Here are nine basic embroidery stitches used in this book.
I'll also show you tricks for finishing your work beautifully.

Straight Stitch

This stitch is for creating short lines. The number of strands you use will produce a different effect.

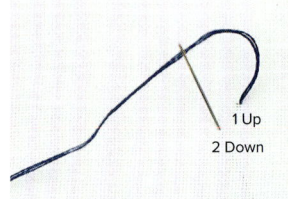

1 Up
2 Down

Running Stitch

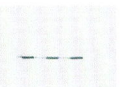

This stitch creates a dotted line. Once you get the knack for this stitch, you can really run with it.

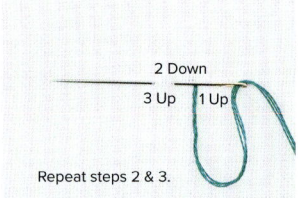

2 Down
3 Up   1 Up
Repeat steps 2 & 3.

Outline Stitch

Use this for borders, as well as for stems and branches. This stitch creates a beautiful finish when sewing on an intricate curve.

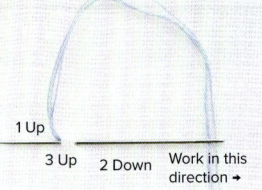

1 Up
3 Up   2 Down   Work in this direction ➜

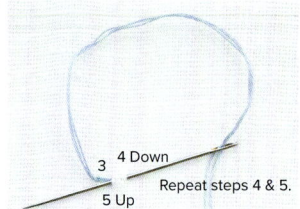

3   4 Down
5 Up   Repeat steps 4 & 5.

Chain Stitch

Use this stitch for lines or for filling in areas. To create a plump and pretty chain stitch, don't pull the thread too tight and keep the size of the loops uniform.

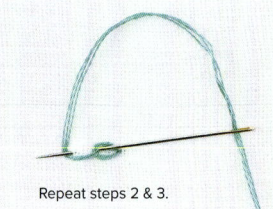

2 Down
3 Up   1 Up

Repeat steps 2 & 3.

TIP
When filling in an area, be careful not to leave any gaps.

French Knot Stitch

The basic French knot stitch is a double wrap. Adjust the size based on the number of strands of thread. The knots are easily crushed, so work them as you finish a project.

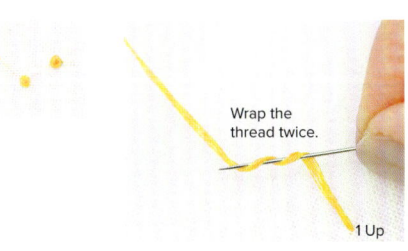

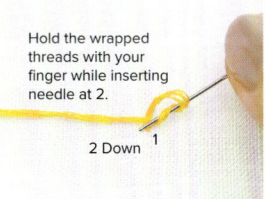

Wrap the thread twice.

1 Up

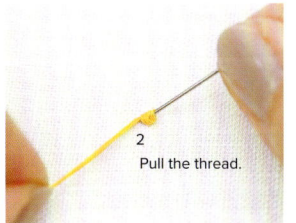

Hold the wrapped threads with your finger while inserting needle at 2.

2 Down   1

2

Pull the thread.

Hold the thread with your finger while pulling it down through the fabric.

Satin Stitch

Work these stitches side by side to fill in an area. To create a beautiful finish, line up the parallel threads and make sure they aren't twisted.

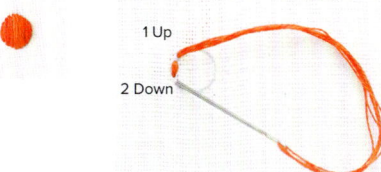

1 Up

2 Down

Repeat steps 1 & 2.

Long and Short Stitch

Work alternating long and short stitches side by side to fill in an area. Use this stitch for things such as fan-shaped flower petals.

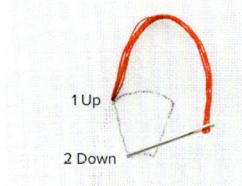

1 Up

2 Down

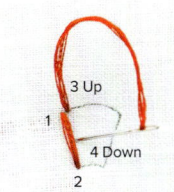

3 Up

1

4 Down

2

5 Up

2 6 Down

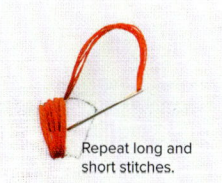

Repeat long and short stitches.

Lazy Daisy Stitch

This stitch creates a small flower petal or leaf. Maintain a full shape by not pulling the thread too tightly.

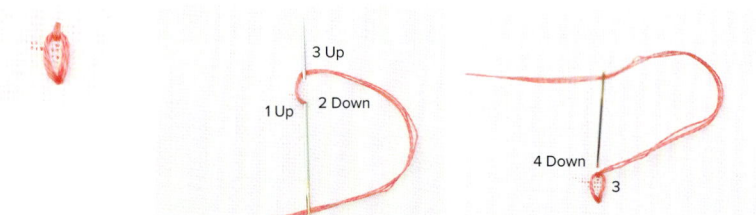

Lazy Daisy Stitch + Straight Stitch

Sew one or two straight stitches across the center of the lazy daisy. It creates a full oval shape. You can adjust the size depending on the number of strands.

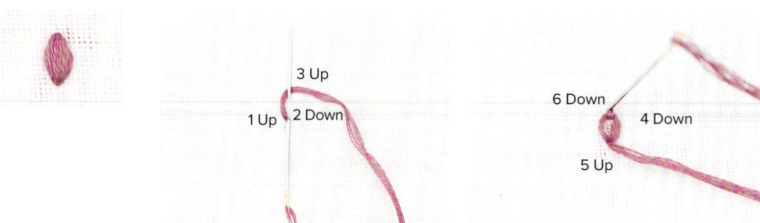

Filling in an Area Neatly (1)

Be careful not to leave any gaps.

1. Sew the outline of the pattern.

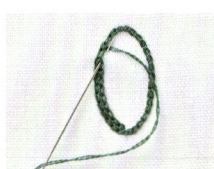

2. Following the outline, sew the additional rows, working from the outside toward the inside. If a gap appears, go back at the end and fill in with more chain stitches or outline stitches.

Filling in an Area Neatly (2)

How to embroider an area that also has an inner border:

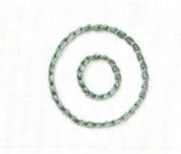

1. Sew both the outer and inner outlines of the pattern.

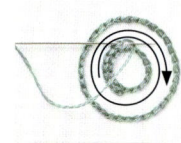

2. Following the inner outline, sew the additional rows, working from the inside toward the outside.

TIPS FOR CHAIN STITCHES
Embroider Neat Angles

To create neat right angles when working chain stitches, the trick is to sew a bit to the inside, as shown, when you turn the angle.

Finish by sewing one stitch.

Embroider Neat Circles

When creating a circle or an outline with chain stitches, make sure to connect the first and last stitches for a clean finish.

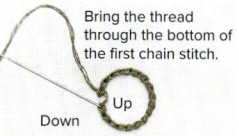

Bring the thread through the bottom of the first chain stitch.

Up

Down

TIPS FOR OUTLINE STITCHES
Embroider Gentle Curves

Bring the needle up and down, then back up halfway between the previous stitch, and repeat. To create an intricate curve, the trick is to make very fine stitches.

OK
When working the needle back up halfway, bring it out above the previous stitch.

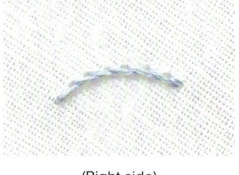

(Right side)

(Reverse side)

NO GOOD
The curve will be imbalanced if the stitches are too big or don't come back up halfway.

(Right side)

(Reverse side)

Embroider Neat Angles

When creating right angles (or close to right angles) using outline stitches, pass the needle through a stitch on the reverse side to keep the thread from coming loose.

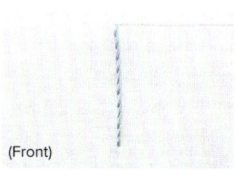

(Front)

1. Sew outline stitches to the corner.

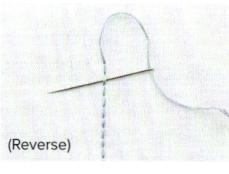

(Reverse)

2. When you turn the angle, pass the needle through a stitch on the reverse side.

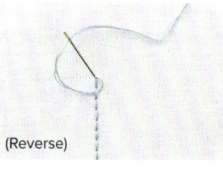

(Reverse)

3. Bring the needle up at the corner on the front side.

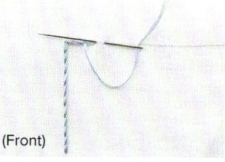

(Front)

4. Continue sewing in the new direction.

Transferring Patterns (1)

First, locate the area where you will transfer the pattern to the fabric. Touch up the fabric with an iron, then arrange the pattern along the warp and weft.

1. Place the tracing paper over the pattern, and transfer the design.

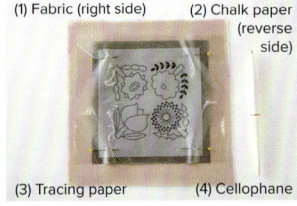

(1) Fabric (right side) (2) Chalk paper (reverse side)

(3) Tracing paper (4) Cellophane

2. Layer as shown in the photo, secure with pins, and trace the pattern using a tracer.

SEE THROUGH A WINDOW . . .

Instead of using a light box, you can also use a window to see through and transfer your pattern. Using masking tape, affix the tracing paper and fabric from step 1 to a window, and you can see right through it!

Transferring Patterns (2)

When transferring large patterns, it can be helpful to use a light box. However, it does not work with thick or dark-colored fabric, in which case refer to "Transferring Patterns (1)."

1. Use a transparent thick-tipped felt pen to transfer the pattern onto tracing paper.

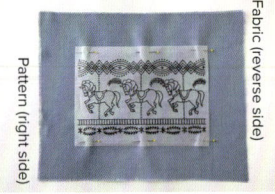

Pattern (right side)

Fabric (reverse side)

2. Layer tracing paper from step 1 over fabric like a photograph and secure with pins.

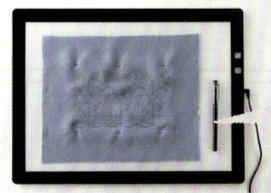

3. Place the fabric with pinned pattern from step 2 facedown on top of the light box, and use a heat erasable fabric marking pen to trace the pattern onto the reverse side of the fabric.

I recommend using a fine-tipped heat erasable fabric marking pen. The roller-ball-type pens can catch on the fabric, making it difficult to trace.

How to Handle Thread (1)

For No. 25 embroidery floss, pull the specified number of strands from the skein, one at a time, then arrange them together with the ends aligned neatly.

1. Pull a standard length of 24" from the skein and cut the thread.

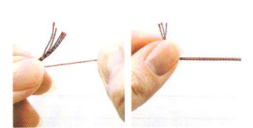

2. One at a time, pull the number of strands you need and arrange them together.

How to Handle Thread (2)

How you thread the desired number of strands through the needle differs depending on whether you're using an odd or even number of strands.

For 6 strands, thread 3 strands through a needle and fold them in half. For 4 strands, thread 2.

For even numbers of strands: For 2 strands, thread 1 length through the needle, fold it in half, align the ends, then make a knot.

For odd numbers of strands: Arrange the desired number of strands, thread the needle, and make a knot at one end.

Knots

Make a knot at the end of the thread when you start stitching embroidery for projects.

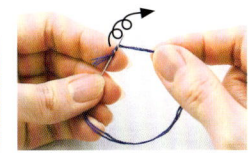

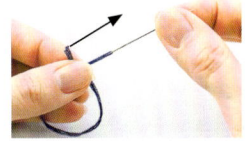

1. Thread the strands through the needle; place the end of the thread near the tip of the needle.

2. Wrap the thread twice around the tip of the needle.

3. Pinch the wrapped thread between your fingertips, slide it down the needle, and pull the knot all the way to the end of the thread.

Starting Your Embroidery (1)

Here's how to start embroidering when creating lines using chain or outline stitches.

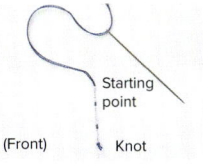

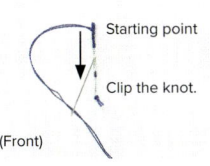

1. Work a few small backstitches along a line toward the starting point, then bring the needle up at the starting point.

2. Continue working, overlaying the stitches from step 1, and when you reach the knot, clip it off.

Starting Your Embroidery (2)

Here's how to start embroidering when filling in areas using satin stitches.

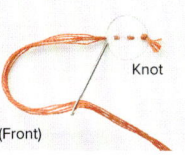

1. Work a few pick stitches (or short running stitches) along a line toward the starting point, then bring the needle up at the starting point.

2. Continue working, covering the stitches from step 1, and when you reach the knot, clip it off.

Finishing Your Embroidery (1)

Here's how to finish embroidering once you've created lines using chain or outline stitches.

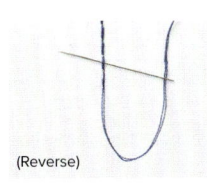

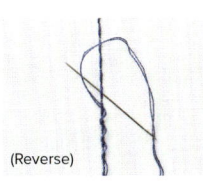

1. Bring the needle up on the reverse side and anchor the thread by wrapping it several times through a stitch on this side.

2. Cut the end of the thread.

Finishing Your Embroidery (2)

Here's how to finish embroidering once you've filled in areas using satin stitches.

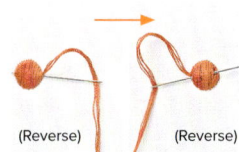

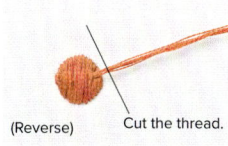

1. Bring the needle up on the reverse side, pass the thread under the stitches several times to anchor the thread.

2. Cut the end of the thread.

When Switching Thread

When you run out of thread or need to switch colors, start a new thread where stitches already exist.

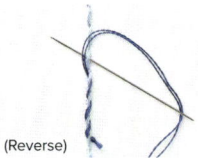

(Reverse)

Weave a knotted length of thread around the stitches on the reverse, and bring the needle up at the starting point. Cut off the knot later.

Completing Your Project

Once you've finished your project, be sure to treat and handle it carefully to help improve the appearance of your finished project.

1. Erase any pattern traces. If the marks are water-soluble, mist water on the reverse side of the fabric, then erase any traces that stick out. Use a moistened cotton swab for tight areas.

2. Touch up with an iron. Use an iron on the reverse side to lightly touch up any wrinkles. Textural stitches are easily damaged, so spread a towel under the project first. Be careful— once ironed, any traces of the ink will become permanent!

TIPS FOR MAKING ZAKKA PROJECTS
Making Neat Seam Allowances on Curved Edges

Making cuts along the curves in the seam allowances for small projects will prevent the fabric from being too stiff when you turn it right side out.

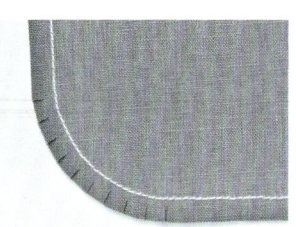

Before turning right side out, make evenly spaced cuts along the curves in the seam allowances. Be careful not to cut the backstitches. (It's best to use pinking shears.)

U-Shaped Ladder Stitch

This stitch is used to close the opening for turning out because it creates an invisible seam.

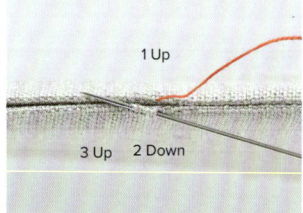

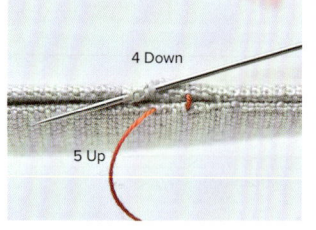

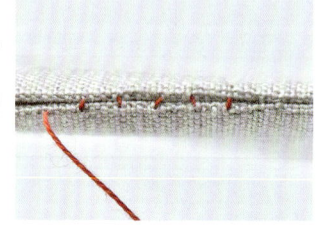

1. Match up the folded edges, and pass the knotted thread through from the reverse side. Insert the needle into the edge facing it, and skim under the fabric of the lower edge.

2. Using the same technique as in step 1, insert the needle into the upper edge directly above, and skim under the fabric.

3. Sew edges together, creating a U shape; finish by tying off a knot and hiding it on the reverse side.

*I used thread in a contrasting color to illustrate here—use thread that matches the right side of your fabric.

Embroidery Patterns and Zakka Project Instructions

This section will introduce you to the 21 patterns and how to stitch them, and includes instructions on how to make the zakka projects that are embroidered with these stitches. I encourage you to pick and choose your favorite motifs from among the patterns, or alternatively you can go big and use them over and over to great effect.

*The number in parentheses is the number of strands, followed by the color code or name for the DMC No. 25 embroidery floss.

*Unless noted otherwise, all numbers in the project instructions refer to inches.

* DMC No. 25 embroidery floss: 168, 640, 920, 950, 3051, 3768, 3778
* For circles, work French knots, unless noted otherwise. For all other stitches, work straight stitch, unless noted otherwise.
* Use 4 strands, unless noted otherwise.
* The number in parentheses is the number of strands, followed by the color code or name for the DMC No. 25 embroidery floss.

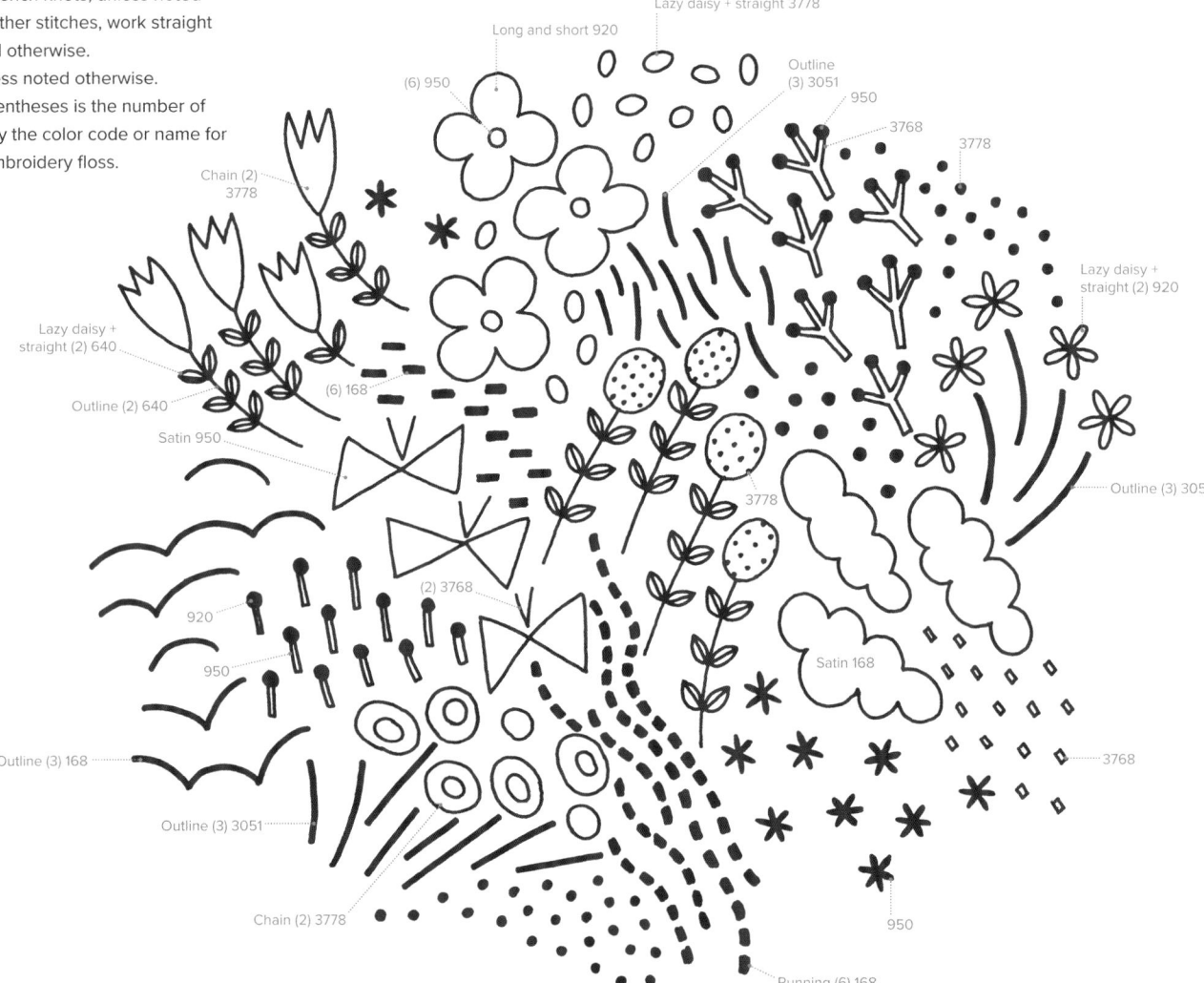

Lazy daisy + straight 3778

Long and short 920

Outline (3) 3051

950

3768

3778

(6) 950

Chain (2) 3778

Lazy daisy + straight (2) 920

Lazy daisy + straight (2) 640

Outline (2) 640

(6) 168

Satin 950

Outline (3) 3051

3778

920

950

(2) 3768

Satin 168

Outline (3) 168

3768

Outline (3) 3051

950

Chain (2) 3778

Running (6) 168

- DMC No. 25 embroidery floss: ecru, 22, 168, 169, 310, 898
- Work outline stitch (4) 898 for thick lines of stems; for all other stitches, work chain stitch (2), unless noted otherwise.
- Use 2 strands, unless noted otherwise.
- The number in parentheses is the number of strands, followed by the color code or name for the DMC No. 25 embroidery floss.

French knot (6) 22

Long and short (4) ecru

Satin (4) 22

Work satin stitches (4) 169 over chain stitches.

Ecru

Ecru

Work straight stitches (4) 310 over chain stitches.

Straight ecru

Outline 168

898

22

Lazy daisy + straight (4) 169

Outline (1) 898

Straight (4) 310

Straight 168

* DMC No. 25 embroidery floss: 733, 829, 932, 950, 3042, 3832, 3850
* Work chain stitch (2), unless noted otherwise.
* Use 2 strands, unless noted otherwise.
* The number in parentheses is the number of strands, followed by the color code or name for the DMC No. 25 embroidery floss.

Straight (4) 733

Satin (4) 932

French knot 3832

Outline (1) 3832 *Work straight stitches (1) for short lines.

Outline 829

3850

Lazy daisy + straight 3850

3042

Straight (4) 733

Satin (4) 3832

French knot (6) 950

Satin (4) 829

Work French knot stitches (4) 829 over chain stitches for clothing.

Straight 829

950

3832

Ribbons / page 16

* DMC No. 25 embroidery floss: 01, 04, 150, 3687
* Work outline (2) for all stitches.

* DMC No. 25 embroidery floss: 224, 310, 501, 611, 645, 733, 932, 3865
* Work outline stitch, unless noted otherwise.
* Use 2 strands, unless noted otherwise.
* The number in parentheses is the number of strands, followed by the color code or name for the DMC No. 25 embroidery floss.

French knot (4) 733

224

Straight (4) 3865

Straight 3865

733

3865

Satin (4) 224

645

French knot 645

733

Satin (4) 611

Chain 310

Straight (4) 611

Straight 645

Work all of these stitches over chain stitches.

Work satin stitches (4) 611 over chain stitches.

Chain 645

French knot (4) alternating 932 with 3865

Straight (4) 932

932

French knot (4) 224

Straight (4) 501

(1) 501

Lazy daisy + straight 3865

Soil and Roots / page 20

* DMC No. 25 embroidery floss: 310, 319, 502, 833, 986, 3033, 3363, 3790, 3865
* Work outline stitch, unless noted otherwise.
* Use 2 strands, unless noted otherwise.
* The number in parentheses is the number of strands, followed by the color code or name for the DMC No. 25 embroidery floss.

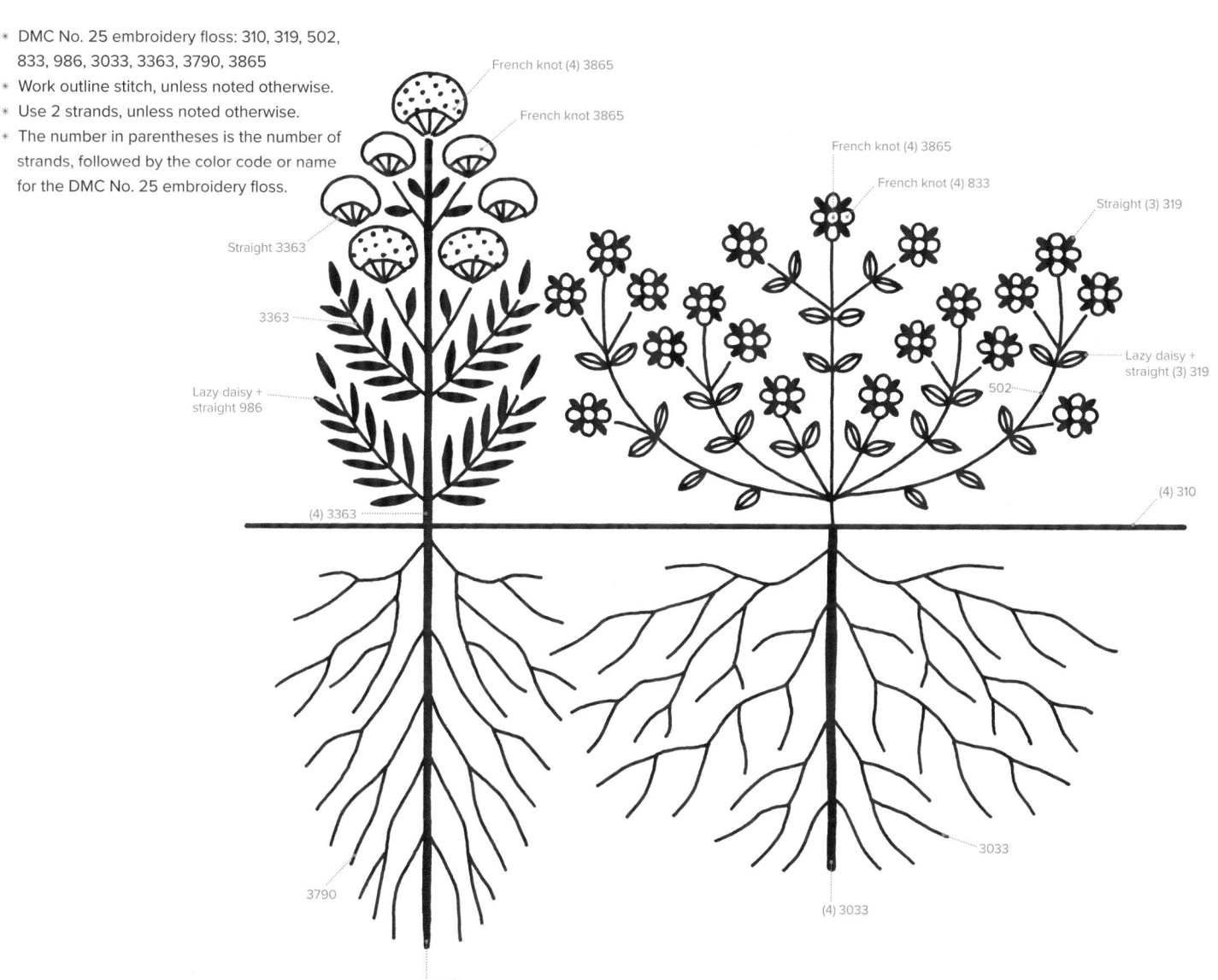

French knot (4) 3865

French knot 3865

French knot (4) 3865

French knot (4) 833

Straight (3) 319

Straight 3363

3363

502

Lazy daisy + straight (3) 319

Lazy daisy + straight 986

(4) 3363

(4) 310

3033

3790

(4) 3033

(4) 3790

Hexagonal Flowers | page 22

* DMC No. 25 embroidery floss: 310, 319, 739, 832, 986 (the coaster uses 3782 in place of 739)
* The number in parentheses is the number of strands, followed by the color code or name for the DMC No. 25 embroidery floss.

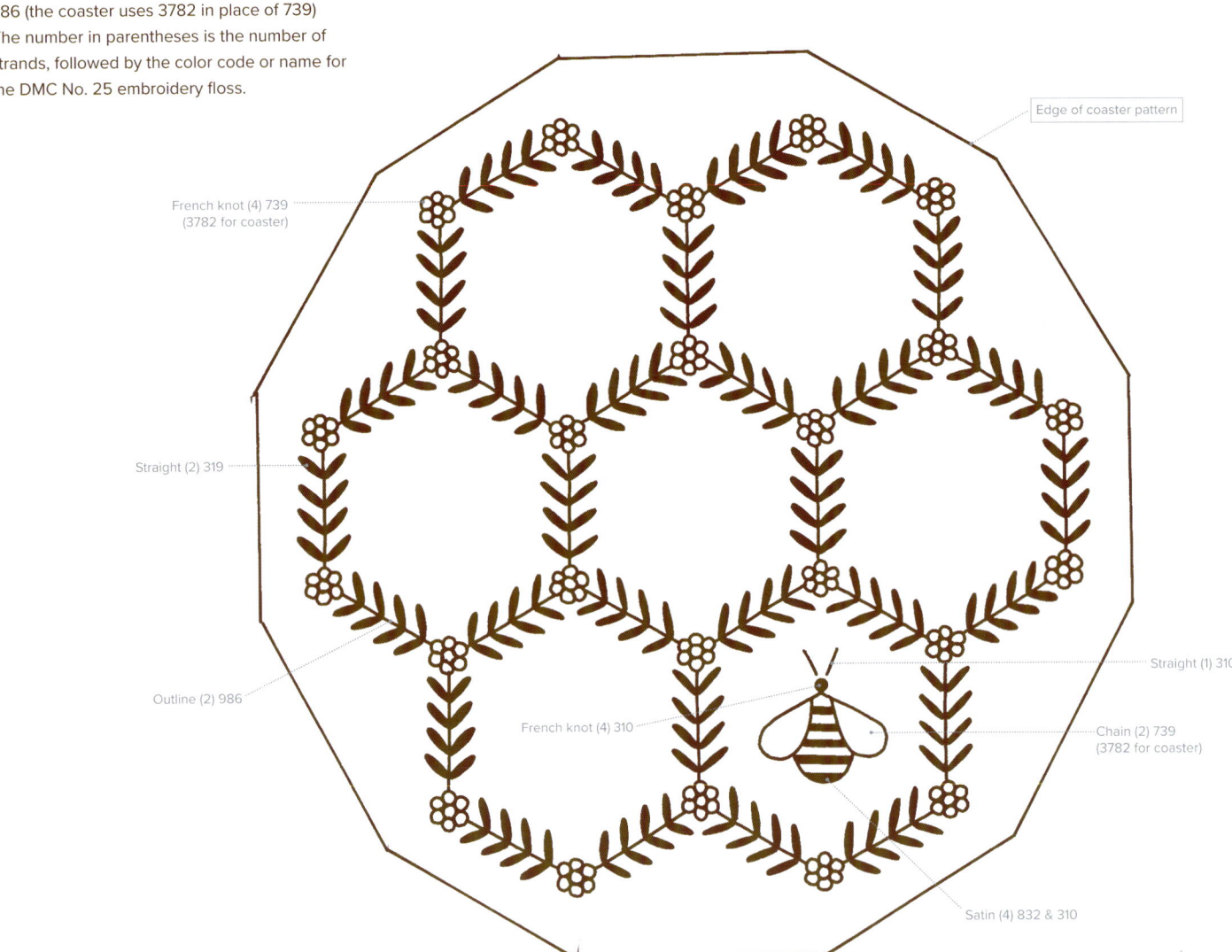

Edge of coaster pattern

French knot (4) 739
(3782 for coaster)

Straight (2) 319

Outline (2) 986

French knot (4) 310

Straight (1) 310

Chain (2) 739
(3782 for coaster)

Satin (4) 832 & 310

Circus / page 24

- DMC No. 25 embroidery floss: 310, 829, 950, 3865
- Work satin stitch (3), unless noted otherwise.
- The number in parentheses is the number of strands, followed by the color code or name for the DMC No. 25 embroidery floss.

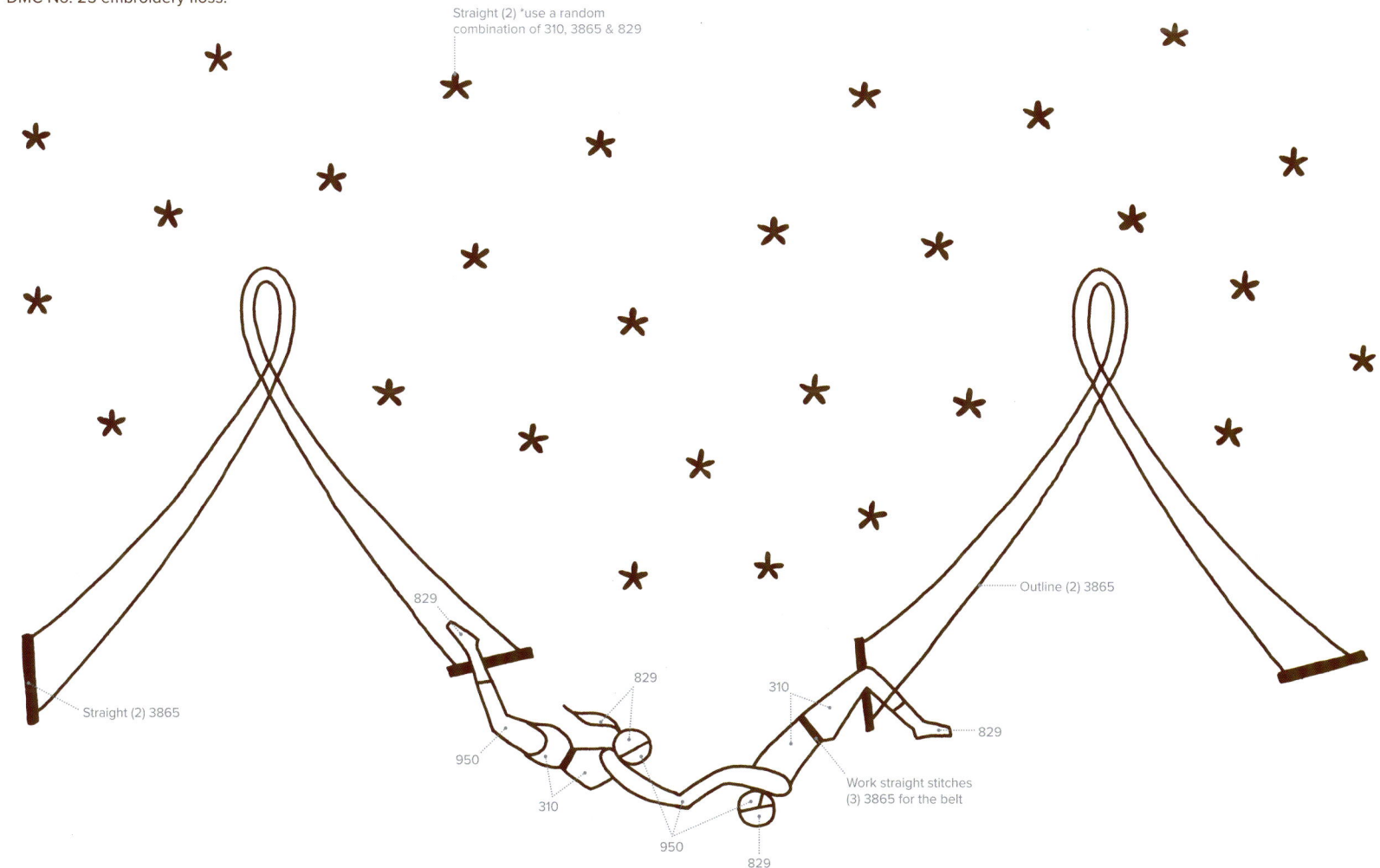

Straight (2) *use a random combination of 310, 3865 & 829

829

829

310

Outline (2) 3865

Straight (2) 3865

950

310

950

829

Work straight stitches (3) 3865 for the belt

* DMC No. 25 embroidery floss: 310, 3866 (the mini pochette uses 05 in place of 3866)
* Work chain stitch (1) 3866, unless noted otherwise.
* Use 1 strand of 3866 for all other stitches.
* The number in parentheses is the number of strands, followed by the color code or name for the DMC No. 25 embroidery floss.

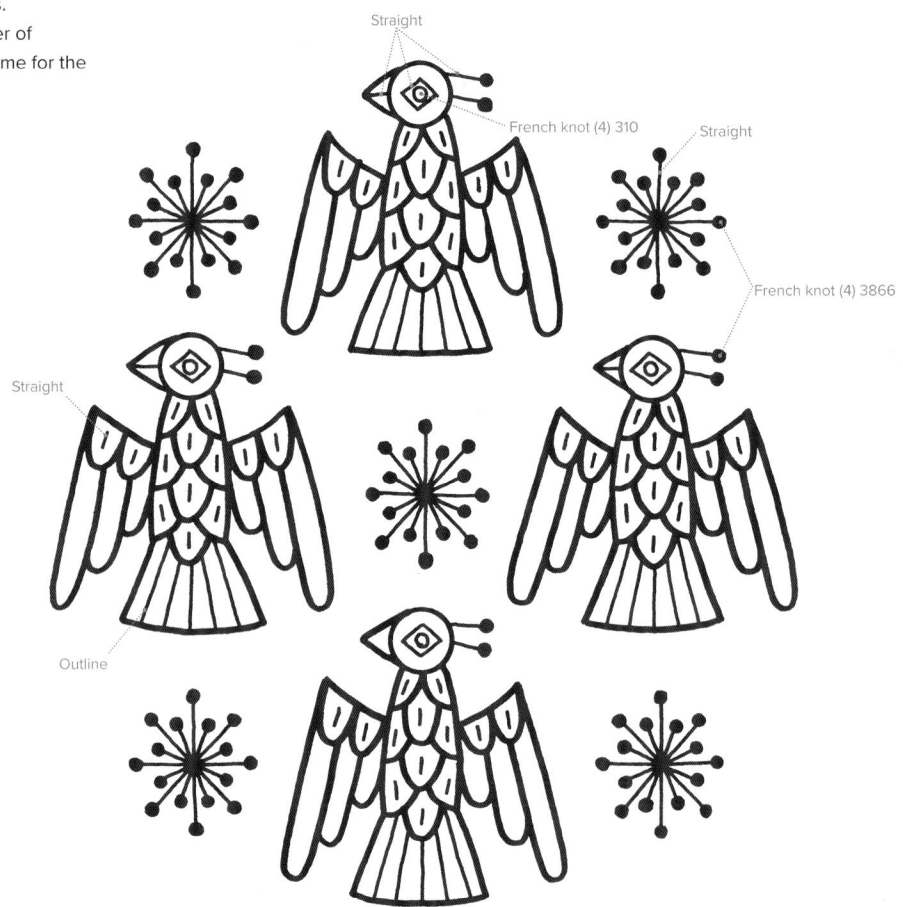

* DMC No. 25 embroidery floss: ecru
* Work outline stitch (2), unless noted otherwise.
* The number in parentheses is the number of
  strands, followed by the color code or name for the
  DMC No. 25 embroidery floss.

Lazy daisy + straight (2)

Outline (1)

French knot (4)

* DMC No. 25 embroidery floss: 733, 3866 (the key case uses 3866 for the stars and 310 for the houses)
* Work outline stitch (1) 3866, unless noted otherwise.
* The number in parentheses is the number of strands, followed by the color code or name for the DMC No. 25 embroidery floss.

Straight (2) 733

French knot (2) 3866

Work straight stitches (2) 3866 for short lines.

Straight (2) 3866   Straight (1) 3866

Work outline stitches (2) 3866 for thick lines.

Roadside / page 32

* DMC No. 25 embroidery floss: 823, 840, 918, 3866
* Work outline stitch (2), unless noted otherwise.
* The number in parentheses is the number of strands, followed by the color code or name for the DMC No. 25 embroidery floss.

Lazy daisy + straight (3) 918

840

Satin (4) 840

French knot (6) 823

Outline (6) 823

823

840

Work straight stitches (2) 3866 for short lines.

Straight (6) 3866

3866

French knot (6) 3866

Edge of bookmark pattern

* DMC No. 25 embroidery floss: 739, 833, 869, 895, 3346
* Work outline stitch (2), unless noted otherwise.
* The number in parentheses is the number of
  strands, followed by the color code or name for
  the DMC No. 25 embroidery floss.

Edge of crown pattern

3346

895

Lazy daisy +
straight (4) 895

869

895

French knot (4) 833

French knot (4) 739

869

Satin (4) 3346

3346

Festive Flowers | page 36

* DMC No. 25 embroidery floss: 522, 600, 834, 904, 962, 986, 3755, 3847, 3865
* Work outline stitch, unless noted otherwise.
* The number in parentheses is the number of strands, followed by the color code or name for the DMC No. 25 embroidery floss.

(2) 522
French knot (3) 3865
French knot (2) 600
(1) 600
(1) 3847
Lazy daisy + straight (3) 834
Chain (1) 986
Lazy daisy + straight (2) 3847
French knot (3) 834
Straight (1) 986
Lazy daisy + straight (3) 3865
French knot (4) 3755
(1) 522
Satin (4) 522
Chain (1) 986
Lazy daisy + straight (3) 962
(2) 986
Chain (1) 904
(2) 904

Satin (4) 501
Long and short (6) 3866
Lazy daisy + straight (4) 502
Outline (2) 502
French knot (6) 832
501
Satin (4) 502
554
Long and short (4) 501
Satin (4) 739
French knot (6) 739
Straight (2) 739
3755
739
931
Satin (4) 502
501
Satin (4) 501

Four Seasons of Flowers | page 42

* DMC No. 25 embroidery floss: 501, 502, 554, 739, 832, 931, 3755, 3866
* Work chain stitch (2), unless noted otherwise.
* The number in parentheses is the number of strands, followed by the color code or name for the DMC No. 25 embroidery floss.

- DMC No. 25 embroidery floss: 561, 840, 3033, 3722, 3799 (for the shoulder bag, use 3033 for all stitches)
- Work chain stitch (2) 3799 for the outlines and work satin stitch (6) to fill in areas.
- For the shoulder bag, omit filling in the outlines.
- The number in parentheses is the number of strands, followed by the color code or name for the DMC No. 25 embroidery floss.

840

561

840

840

Straight (4) 3799

Use 3033 for white flowers & use 3722 for pink flowers.

Work straight stitches (4) 3799 over satin stitches.

- DMC No. 25 embroidery floss: 28, 223, 224, 500, 647, 3721, 3866
- Work outline stitch (3) 647 for thick lines.
- Use 2 strands, unless noted otherwise.
- The number in parentheses is the number of strands, followed by the color code or name for the DMC No. 25 embroidery floss.

Satin (4) 223

French knot 224

French knot (4) 28

Outline 647

Lazy daisy + straight (4) 500

Outline 647

Lazy daisy + straight (6) 3721

Straight (4) 500

French knot (6) 224

Outline 500

French knot (4) 3866

Lazy daisy + straight 223

Lazy daisy + straight 500

Chain 500

Outline 500

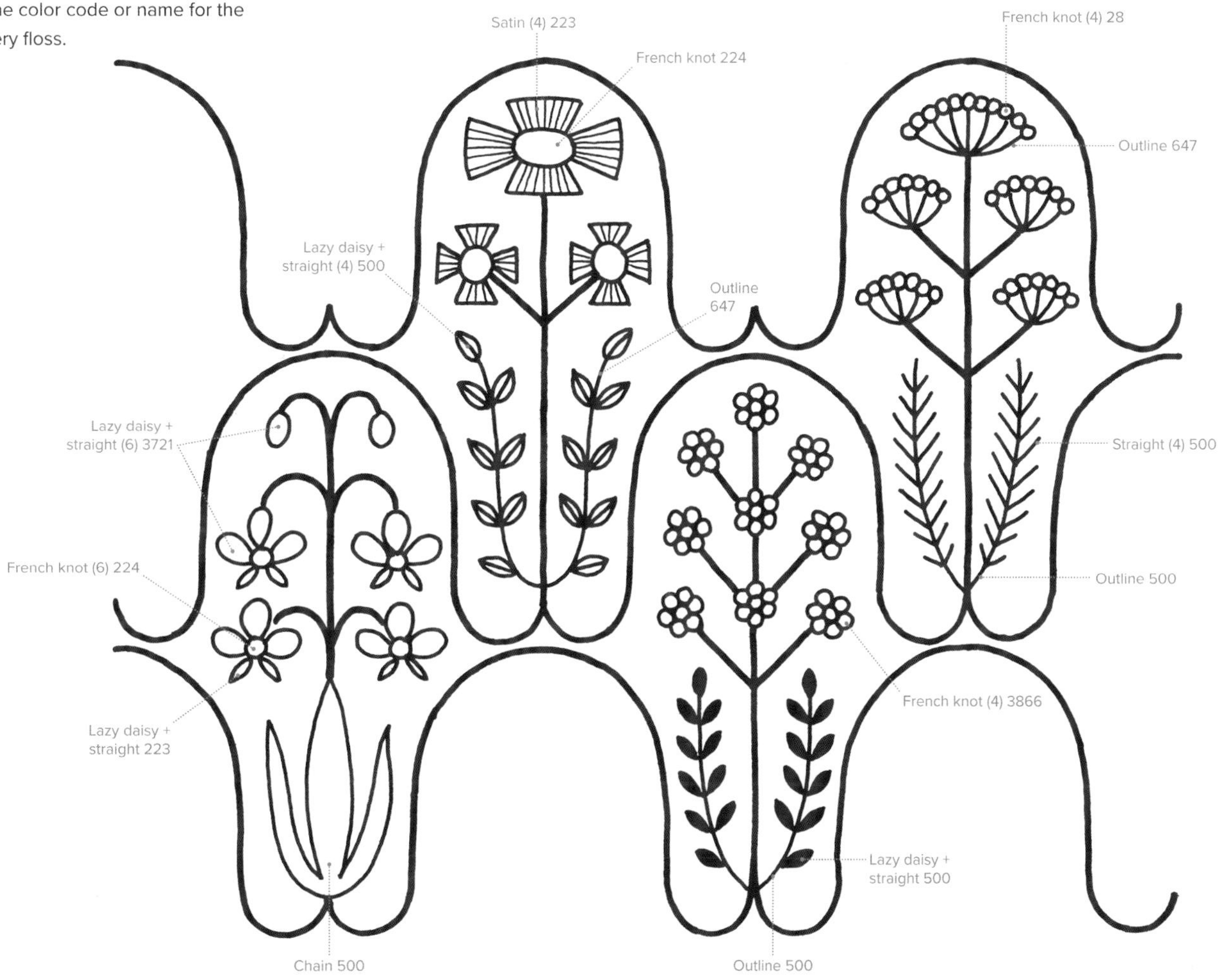

* DMC No. 25 embroidery floss: 3777 (use 610 for bracelet)
* Work outline stitch (2), unless noted otherwise.
* The number in parentheses is the number of strands, followed by the color code or name for the DMC No. 25 embroidery floss.

Edge of bracelet pattern

Lazy daisy + straight (3)

Straight (4)

Work straight stitches (4) for center stems.

Attach bracelet's loop here.

French knot (2)

French knot (4)

Chain (2)

- DMC No. 25 embroidery floss: 02, 310, 645, 924, 926 (for the tea cozy, use 3024 for all stitches)
- Use 4 strands, unless noted otherwise.
- For the tea cozy, work outline (1) for all stitches that aren't noted as straight (4).
- The number in parentheses is the number of strands, followed by the color code or name for the DMC No. 25 embroidery floss.

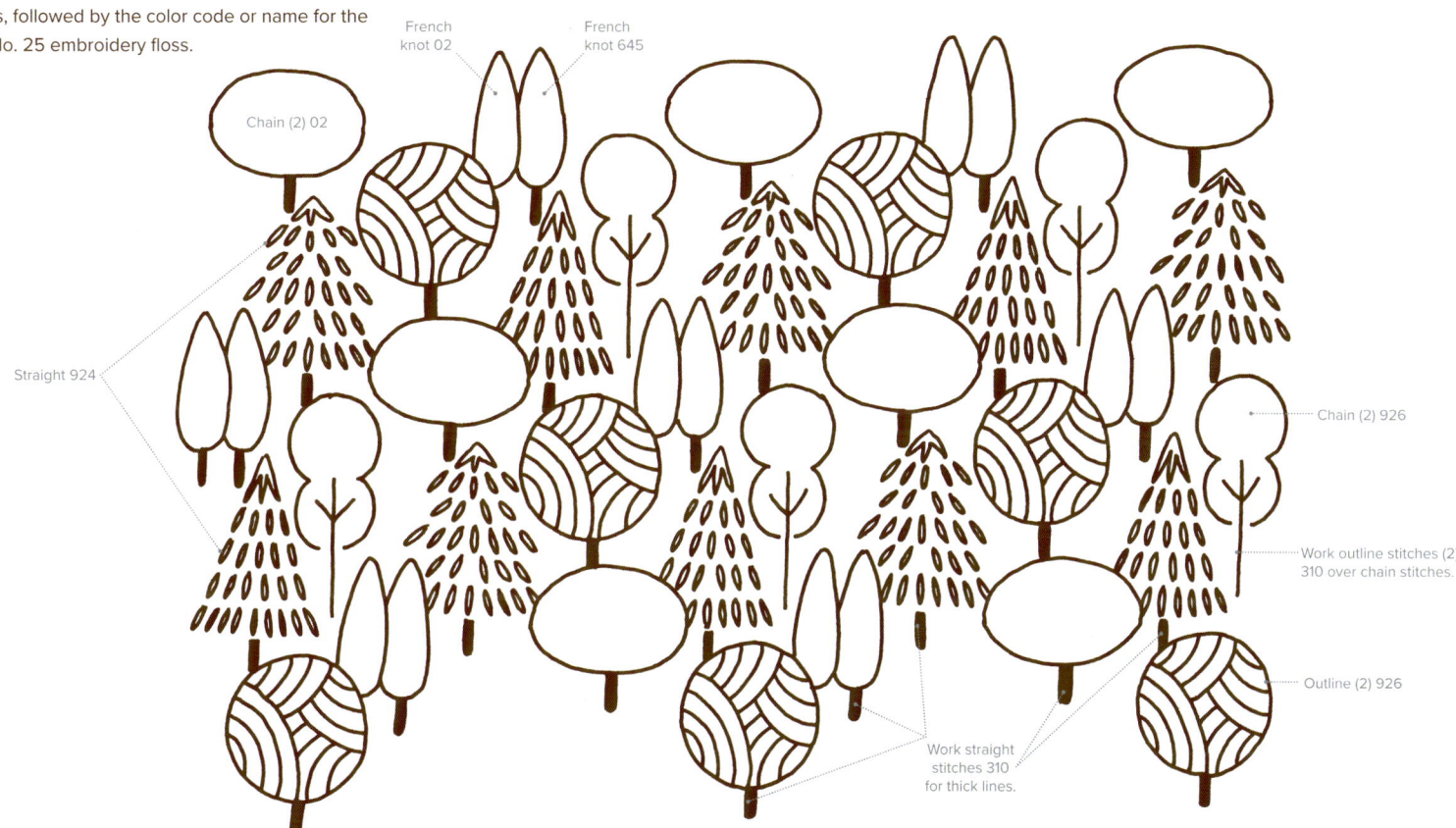

French knot 02

French knot 645

Chain (2) 02

Straight 924

Chain (2) 926

Work outline stitches (2) 310 over chain stitches.

Outline (2) 926

Work straight stitches 310 for thick lines.

* DMC No. 25 embroidery floss: 310, 520, 646, 733, 919, 3865
* Work satin stitch, unless noted otherwise.
* Use 2 strands, unless noted otherwise.
* The number in parentheses is the number of strands, followed by the color code or name for the DMC No. 25 embroidery floss.

Song

CLOCK | page 11

Finished size: 8½" diameter

* DMC No. 25 embroidery floss: 168, 640, 920, 950, 3051, 3768, 3778, 1 skein each

Materials

Fabric: Linen, red, 13¾" x 13¾"

Quilt batting, 9¾" x 9¾"

Hand-quilting thread (your choice of color), about 31½"

Clock base (round, wood), 8½" diameter, ½" thick

Quartz clock movement, 1 piece

*Use a long shaft (for ⅛"–¾" clock face)

Wall-mount hook, 1 piece

Rubber O-ring, 1 piece

Clock hand nut, 1 piece

Clock hands (hour, minute, second), 1 each

How to Make

Transfer the embroidery pattern (full-size pattern insert, side A), centered, onto the right side of the exterior fabric. Embroider the pattern (embroidery instructions on p. 60), and iron your work lightly. Align the finished embroidery at the center of the clock base and cut the fabric, adding a 2⅜" seam allowance all the way around. It's a good idea to use pinking shears.

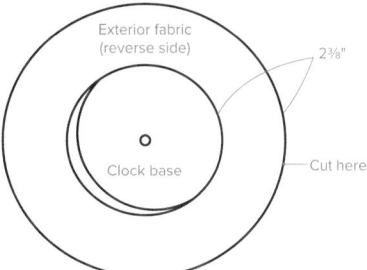

Using the hand-quilting thread, work pick stitches (or short running stitches) around the finished work, about ¾" from the edge. Leave the needle and thread as is.

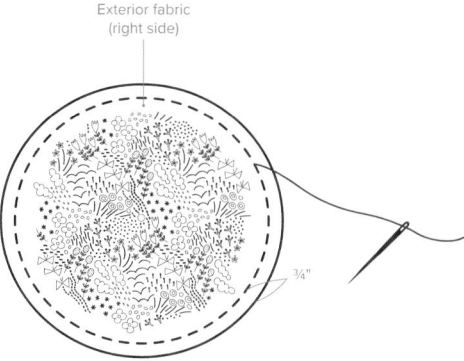

Cut the quilt batting to the same dimensions as the clock base. Assemble the quilt batting and the clock base, centered together, on the reverse side of the exterior fabric, and then pull tightly on the pick stitches to gather the fabric.

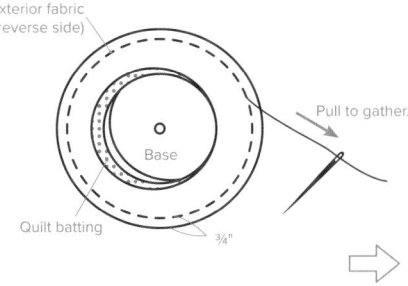

Assemble the clock in the order shown in the diagram. Make a small hole in the center of the embroidered fabric and pass the quartz movement with the wall-mount hook and rubber O-ring attached through the center hole of the clock base. Attach the clock hand nut to the front and secure, then fasten the clock hands in the order shown. Lastly, insert a battery and set the time on the clock.

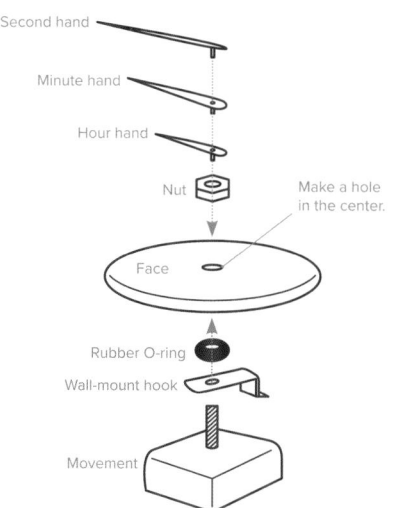

The Life Cycle of an Apple

KITCHEN MITT | page 13

Finished size: 7" x 11" (for right-hand use)

* DMC No. 25 embroidery floss: ecru, 22, 168, 310, 898, 1 skein each
* DMC 169, 2 skeins

Materials

Exterior fabric: Linen, light blue, 15¾" x 19¾"

Lining: Quilt cloth, 15¾" x 19¾"

Loop fabric: Linen, light blue, 4" x 1½"

Machine-sewing thread, light blue, as needed

How to Make

Using an iron, press folds into the fabric for the loop, as shown, and machine stitch the edge.

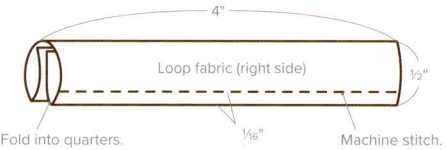

Fold into quarters. — Loop fabric (right side) — 4" — ½" — 1/16" — Machine stitch.

Transfer the pattern (full-size pattern insert, side A) to the right side of the exterior (this will be the back of the hand). Embroider the pattern (embroidery instructions on p. 61), and iron your work lightly. Transfer the mitt pattern to the reverse side, then cut out, adding a ½" seam allowance. Prepare another piece of exterior fabric for the palm of the hand the same way. Transfer the mitt pattern to the lining fabric, and cut two pieces.

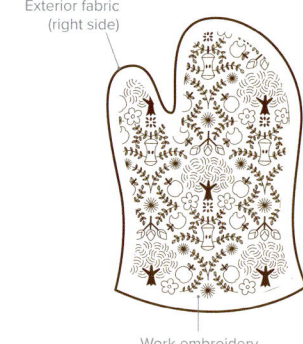

Exterior fabric (right side)

Work embroidery.

Assemble the exterior fabric from step 2 with right sides together. Fold and insert the loop from step 1 in between these at the attachment mark, with the fold toward the inside, and sew together, leaving the opening for the hand. Trim the seam allowances to ¼" and make cuts along the curves. Sew the lining fabric together in the same way, leaving an opening for turning out.

> ### LINING THE MITT WITH QUILT CLOTH
> The thickness of quilt cloth means that if you cut the lining to the same dimensions as the exterior fabric, the excess material will be too puffy. By slightly reducing the size of the lining fabric (approximately 1/16" smaller than the exterior fabric), your finished project will have a beautiful shape.

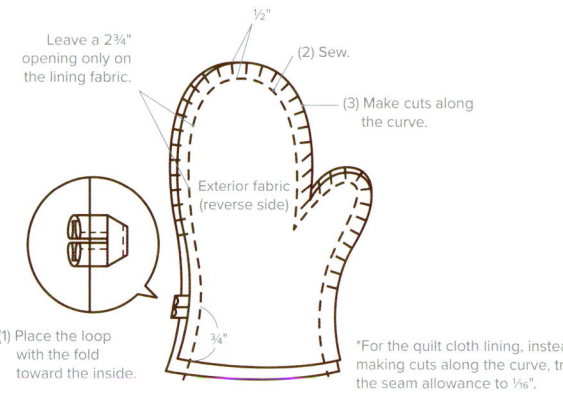

Leave a 2¾" opening only on the lining fabric.

½"

(2) Sew.

(3) Make cuts along the curve.

Exterior fabric (reverse side)

(1) Place the loop with the fold toward the inside.

¾"

*For the quilt cloth lining, instead of making cuts along the curve, trim the seam allowance to 1/16".

Insert the exterior fabric inside the lining fabric from step 3, right sides together, and sew together along the bottom edge. Turn right side out, and lightly iron to reshape. With a U-shaped ladder stitch, sew the opening closed.

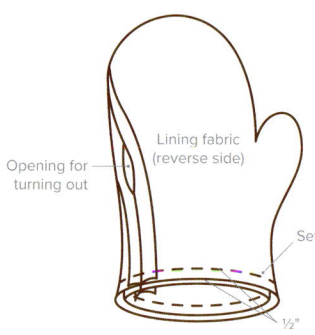

Opening for turning out

Lining fabric (reverse side)

Sew.

½"

Chatty Girls

SANITARY CASE | page 15

Finished size: 4¾" x 4¾"

* DMC No. 25 embroidery floss: 733, 829, 932, 950, 3042, 3832, 3850, 1 skein each

Materials

Exterior fabric: Linen, pale pink, 7⅞" x 11¾"

Lining: Linen, white, 7⅞" x 25¾"

½"-wide ribbon, 11¾" long, 2 pieces

Machine-sewing thread, pale pink, as needed

How to Make

Transfer the embroidery pattern (p. 62) onto the right side of the exterior fabric. Embroider the pattern, and iron your work lightly. Trace the finished dimensions onto the reverse side, and cut the fabric, adding a ½" seam allowance on all four sides.

For the lining fabric, trace the finished dimensions and cut out, adding a ½" seam allowance all around.

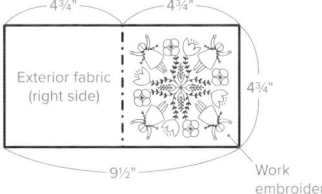

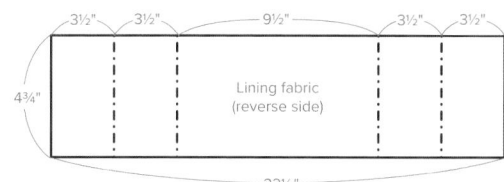

Assemble the exterior fabric and the lining fabric, as shown, right sides together and with the ribbon inserted in between, and sew together.

Arrange the lining fabric, as shown, with 3½" folds on both sides, and sew along the top and bottom edges, leaving an opening for turning out.

Turn right side out, and lightly iron to reshape. With a U-shaped ladder stitch, sew the opening closed.

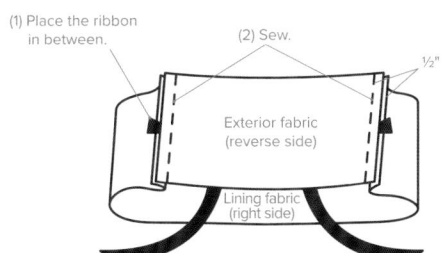

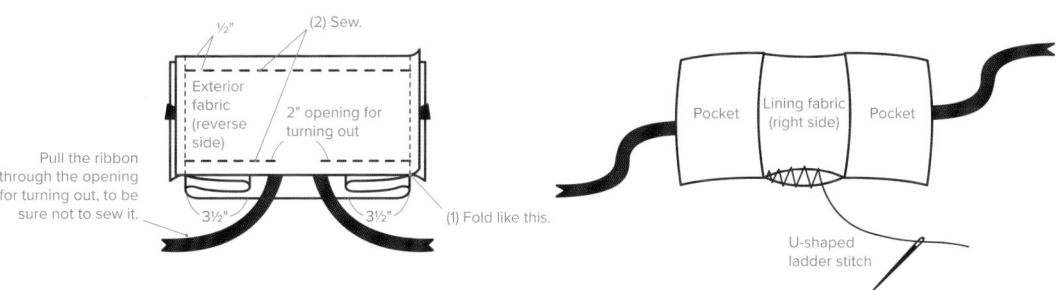

Ribbons

GIFT BAG | page 17

Finished size: 6" x 11¾"

* DMC No. 25 embroidery floss: 01, 04, 150, 3687,
  1 skein each

Materials

Exterior fabric: Linen, black, 7⅞" x 15¾"

Lining: Linen, black, 7⅞" x 15¾"

½"-wide velvet ribbon, black, 13¾" long, 2 pieces

Machine-sewing thread, black, as needed

How to Make

1

Transfer the embroidery pattern (p. 63) onto the right side of the exterior fabric. Embroider the pattern, and iron your work lightly. Trace the finished dimensions onto the reverse side, as shown, and cut the fabric, adding a ½" seam allowance on all four sides. Cut the lining fabric in the same way.

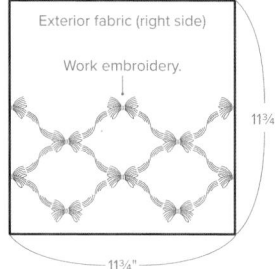

Exterior fabric (right side)

Work embroidery.

11¾"

11¾"

2

Fold the exterior fabric in half, right sides together, and with the ribbon placed in between at the attachment mark, 3⅛" from the top edge, sew together. Press seam allowances open. Sew the lining fabric together in the same way, leaving an opening for turning out.

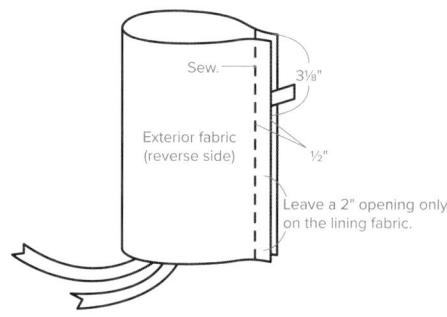

Sew.

3⅛"

Exterior fabric (reverse side)

½"

Leave a 2" opening only on the lining fabric.

3

Refold the exterior bag so that the seam is centered, and sew the bottom edges together. Sew the interior bag in the same way.

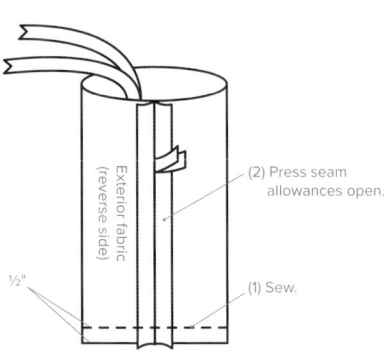

Exterior fabric (reverse side)

(2) Press seam allowances open.

½"

(1) Sew.

4

Assemble the exterior bag and interior bag, right sides together, and sew around the mouth of the bag.

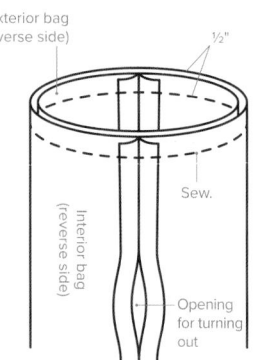

Exterior bag (reverse side)

½"

Interior bag (reverse side)

Sew.

Opening for turning out

5

Turn right side out, and lightly iron to reshape. With a U-shaped ladder stitch, sew the opening closed.

Merry-Go-Round

OBLONG POUCH | page 19

Finished size: 7⅞" x 5¼"

* DMC No. 25 embroidery floss: 224, 310, 501, 611, 645, 733, 932, 3865, 1 skein each

Materials

Exterior fabric: Linen, blue, 9¾" x 17¾"

Lining 1: Linen, blue, 9¾" x 6"

Lining 2: Linen, white, 9¾" x 11¾"

¼"-wide cord, 2⅜" long, 1 piece

⅝"-diameter button, 1 piece

Machine-sewing thread, white, as needed

How to Make

1

Transfer the embroidery pattern (p. 64) onto the right side of the exterior fabric. Embroider the pattern, and iron your work lightly. Trace the finished dimensions onto the reverse side, as shown below, and cut the fabric, adding a ½" seam allowance on all four sides.

2

For the lining fabrics, trace the finished dimensions and cut out, adding a ½" seam allowance on all four sides.

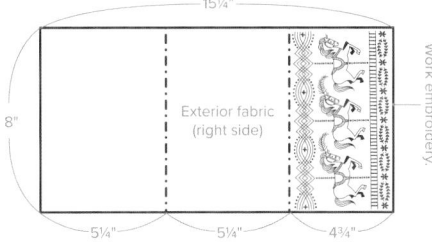

15¼"

8"

Exterior fabric (right side)

Work embroidery.

5¼"   5¼"   4¾"

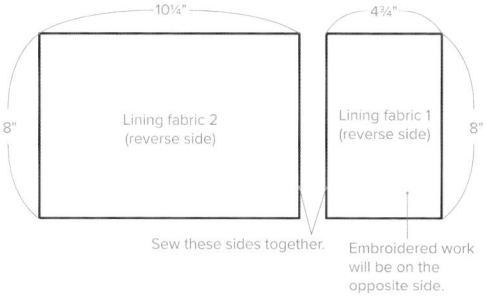

10¼"   4¾"

8"

Lining fabric 2 (reverse side)

Lining fabric 1 (reverse side)

8"

Sew these sides together.

Embroidered work will be on the opposite side.

3

Assemble the lining fabrics from step 2 with right sides together, and sew them together on one side, ½" from the edge of each piece. Press the seam allowances open.

4

Assemble the exterior fabric from step 1 and the lining fabric from step 3, right sides together. Fold the cord in half and insert it, with the fold toward the inside, in between the exterior and lining fabrics at the attachment mark, and sew both sides together.

5

Fold the longer side of step 4 inward, as shown, and sew together along the top and bottom edges, leaving an opening for turning out.

6

Turn right side out, and lightly iron to reshape. With a U-shaped ladder stitch, sew the opening closed. Sew on the button.

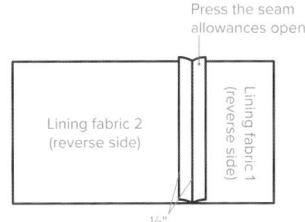

Press the seam allowances open.

Lining fabric 2 (reverse side)

Lining fabric 1 (reverse side)

½"

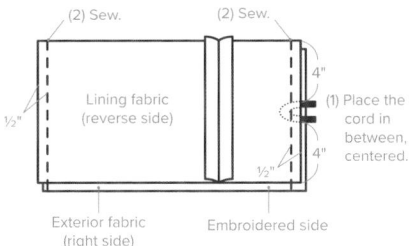

(2) Sew.   (2) Sew.

½"

Lining fabric (reverse side)

4"

(1) Place the cord in between, centered.

½"   4"

Exterior fabric (right side)

Embroidered side

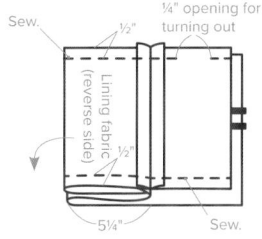

Sew.   ½"   ¼" opening for turning out

Lining fabric (reverse side)

½"

5¼"   Sew.

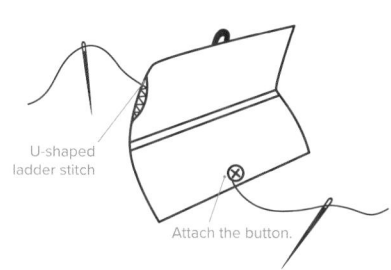

U-shaped ladder stitch

Attach the button.

Soil and Roots

PLANTER COVER | page 21

Finished size: 9¾" H x 4" W x 7⅞" L

* DMC No. 25 embroidery floss: 310, 319, 502, 833, 986, 3033, 3363, 3790, 3865, 1 skein each

Materials

Exterior fabric: Linen, camel, 17¾" x 11¾"

Lining: Linen, white, 17¾" x 11¾"

Loop fabric: Linen, camel, 4¾" x 1½"

One-sided fusible quilt batting (soft, lightweight), 16" x 9¾"

Machine-sewing thread, camel, as needed

How to Make

Using an iron, press folds into the fabric for the loop, as shown, and machine stitch the edge.

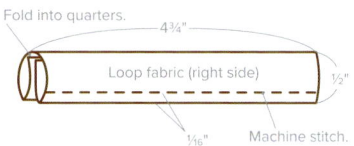

Transfer the embroidery pattern (p. 65) onto the right side of the exterior fabric. Embroider the pattern, and iron your work lightly. Trace the finished dimensions onto the reverse side, as shown, and cut the fabric, adding a ½" seam allowance all around. Cut the lining fabric in the same way.

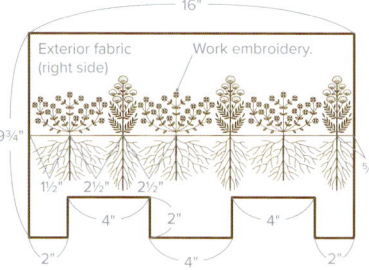

Cut the one-sided fusible quilt batting to the dimensions shown below. Place the fusible side of the quilt batting on the reverse side of the embroidered work, and if you're using a pressing cloth, lay that on top before using an iron to activate the adhesive.
*Do not attach the quilt batting to the lining fabric.

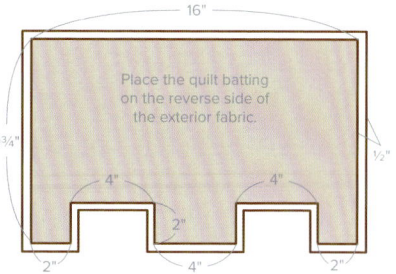

When the fabric from step 3 is cool and the quilt batting has fully adhered, fold the exterior fabric in half, right sides together, and sew the edges together. Sew the lining fabric together in the same way, leaving an opening for turning out.

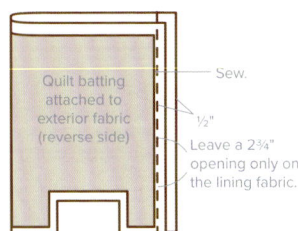

Refold the exterior fabric so that the seam is centered and sew the bottom edge together. Sew the lining fabric in the same way.

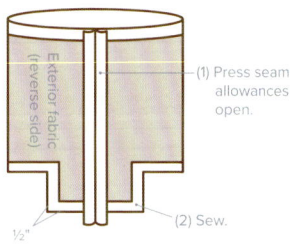

Press the seam allowances on the bottom of the exterior fabric open, then assemble the side and bottom edges like a bag and sew together, as shown. Repeat with the lining fabric.

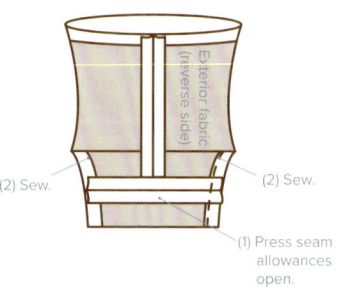

Assemble the interior bag inside the exterior bag, right sides together, then fold and insert the loop in between these, as shown, and sew around the mouth of the bag. Turn right side out, and lightly iron to reshape. With a U-shaped ladder stitch, sew the opening closed.

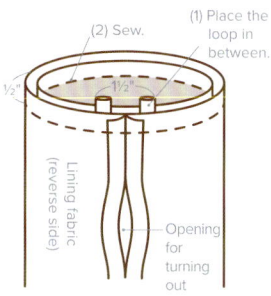

Hexagonal Flowers

COASTER | page 23

Finished size: 5¼" x 5¼"

* DMC No. 25 embroidery floss: 310, 319, 832, 986, 3782, 1 skein each

Materials

Exterior fabric: Linen, white, 7⅞" x 7⅞"

Lining: Linen, white, 7⅞" x 7⅞"

Machine-sewing thread, white, as needed

How to Make

Transfer the embroidery pattern (p. 66) onto the right side of the exterior fabric. Embroider the pattern, and iron your work lightly. Trace the finished dimensions onto the reverse side, and cut the fabric, adding a ½" seam allowance all around. Cut the lining fabric in the same way.

Assemble the exterior fabric and lining fabric, right sides together, and sew together around the edge, leaving an opening for turning out.

Turn right side out, and lightly iron to reshape. With a U-shaped ladder stitch, sew the opening closed.

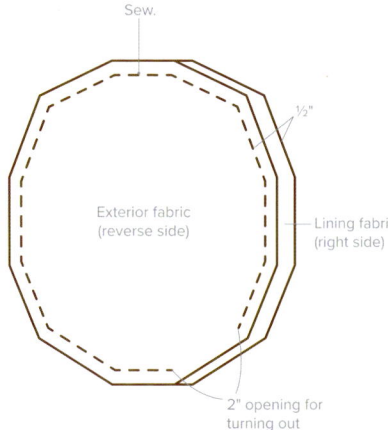

Sew.

½"

Exterior fabric
(reverse side)

Lining fabric
(right side)

2" opening for
turning out

Circus

HANGER COVER | page 25

Finished size: 15¾" x 7½"

* DMC No. 25 embroidery floss: 310, 829, 950, 3865, 1 skein each

Materials

Exterior fabric: Linen, natural, 17¾" x 9¾", 2 pieces

Machine-sewing thread, natural, as needed

Hanger, 1 piece

Tassel: DMC No. 25 embroidery floss ecru, 2 skeins

How to Make

Transfer the embroidery pattern (full-size pattern insert, side A) onto the right side of one of the exterior fabric pieces. Embroider the pattern (embroidery instructions on p. 67), and iron your work lightly. Trace the pattern edges onto the reverse side, and cut the fabric, adding a ½" seam allowance all around. Repeat for the second piece of exterior fabric.

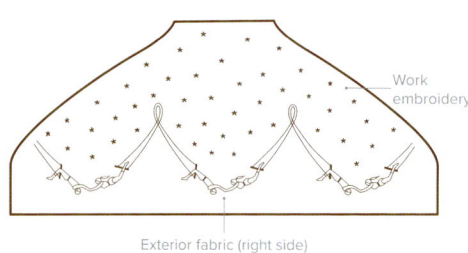

Work embroidery.

Exterior fabric (right side)

On the upper part where the hook of the hanger will come through, fold the seam allowance twice, as shown, and machine stitch the edge. Repeat for the second piece of exterior fabric.

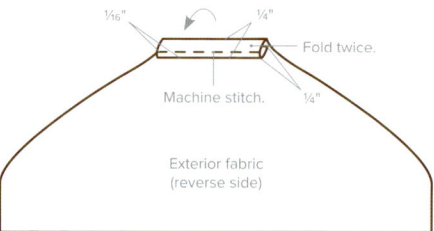

1/16"   1/4"   Fold twice.

Machine stitch.   1/4"

Exterior fabric (reverse side)

Assemble the two exterior fabrics, right sides together, and sew together on both sides. Make cuts along the seam allowances of the curves.

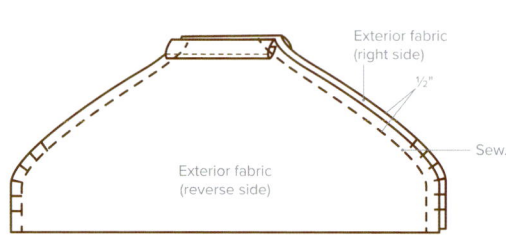

Exterior fabric (right side)

½"

Sew.

Exterior fabric (reverse side)

Turn right side out, and lightly iron to reshape. Along the bottom edge, fold the seam allowances twice, and machine stitch along the edges.

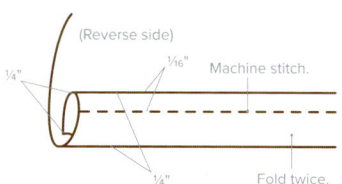

(Reverse side)

1/4"   1/16"   Machine stitch.

1/4"   Fold twice.

Make 7 tassels (see p. 87 for instructions). Insert the hanger from below and sew the tassels onto the bottom edge at regular intervals.

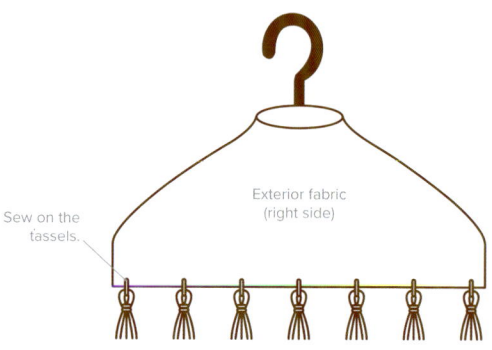

Sew on the tassels.

Exterior fabric (right side)

How to Make the Tassels

Wrap embroidery thread about 20 times around a 1½" piece of cardboard. Cut a 15¾" (approx.) length of embroidery floss and thread it through a needle.

Gently remove the floss from the cardboard, and wrap the thread on the needle around the floss, as if to fasten it. Pull the wrapped thread tight, and pass the needle through the middle.

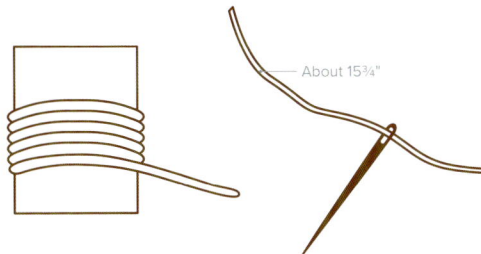

Sew step 2 onto the desired location, and cut the thread.

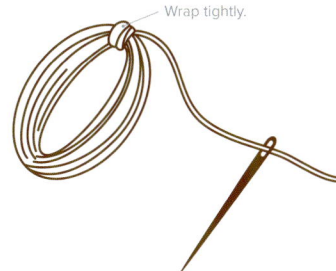

Wrap tightly.

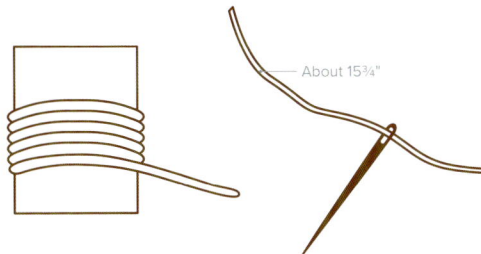

About 15¾"

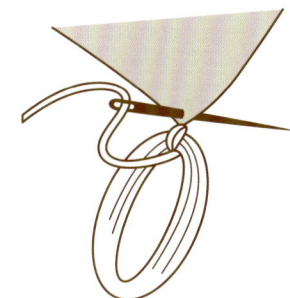

Wrap the thread on the needle around the floss again, ¼" below, pulling the wrapped thread tight, and pass the needle through the middle.

Trim to the desired length with scissors and neaten the threads.

¼"

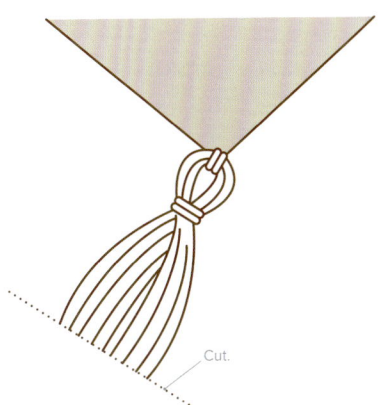

Cut.

Light

MINI POCHETTE | page 27

Finished size: 4¾" x 7⅞"

* DMC No. 25 embroidery floss: 05, 310,
  1 skein each

Materials

Exterior fabric: Linen, dark gray, 7⅞" x 19¾"

Lining fabric: Linen, dark gray, 7⅞" x 19¾"

Shoulder strap fabric: Linen, dark gray, 29½" x 1¼"

One-sided fusible quilt batting (soft, lightweight),
  4¾" x 15¾"

⅝"-wide cord, dark gray, 2⅜", 1 piece

⅝"-diameter button, 1 piece

Machine-sewing thread, dark gray, as needed

How to Make

Using an iron, press folds into the fabric for the shoulder strap, as shown, and machine stitch the edge.

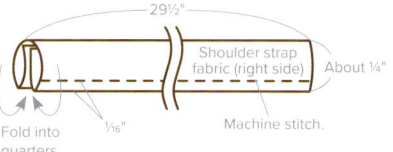

Transfer the embroidery pattern (full-size pattern insert, side A) onto the right side of the exterior fabric. Embroider the pattern (embroidery instructions on p. 68), and iron your work lightly. Trace the finished dimensions onto the reverse side, extending the rectangular pattern as shown, and cut the fabric, adding a ½" seam allowance on all four sides. Cut the lining fabric in the same way.

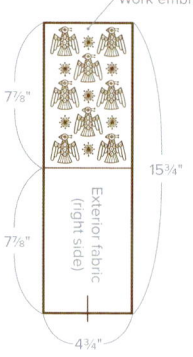

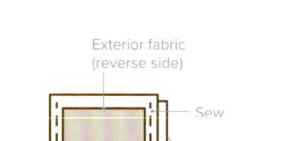

Cut the one-sided fusible quilt batting to the dimensions shown in step 2. Place the fusible side of the quilt batting on the reverse side of the embroidered work, and if you're using a pressing cloth, lay that on top before using an iron to activate the adhesive.
*Do not attach the quilt batting to the lining fabric.

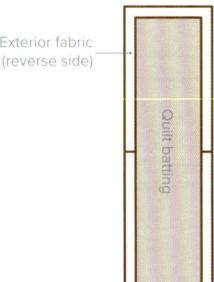

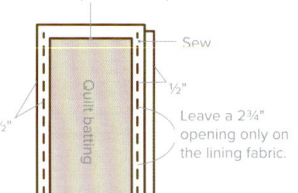

When the fabric from step 3 is cool and the quilt batting has fully adhered, fold the exterior fabric in half, right sides together, and sew the edges together. Sew the lining fabric together in the same way, leaving an opening for turning out.

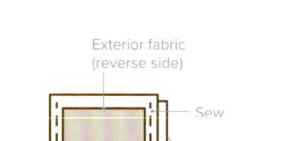

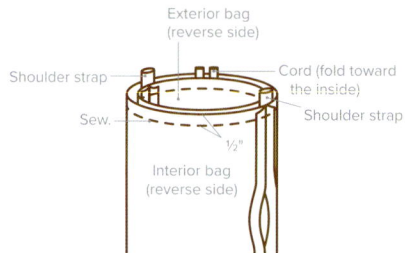

Assemble the exterior bag and interior bag, right sides together. Insert both the cord, folded in half, at the attachment mark, and the shoulder strap from step 1, in between the exterior and interior bags, and sew around the mouth of the bag.
*You can reinforce where the shoulder strap is attached by backstitching several times.

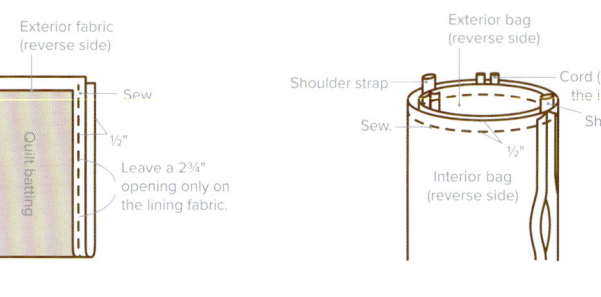

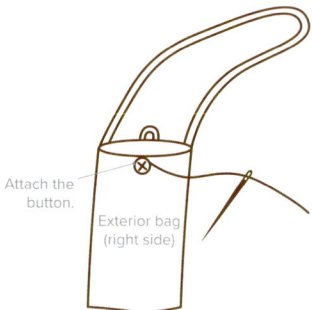

Turn right side out, and lightly iron to reshape. With a U-shaped ladder stitch, sew the opening closed. Sew the button onto the mouth of the bag.

MINI CUSHION | page 29

Finished size: 13¾" x 9¾"

∗ DMC No. 25 embroidery floss: ecru, 3 skeins

Materials

Exterior fabric: Linen, navy blue, 15¾" x 11¾", 2 pieces

Machine-sewing thread, navy blue, as needed

Craft batting, about 12¾ oz (350 g)

Tassel: DMC No. 25 embroidery floss 939, 2 skeins

How to Make

Transfer the embroidery pattern (p. 69) onto the right side of one piece of the exterior fabric. Embroider the pattern, and iron your work lightly. Trace the finished dimensions onto the reverse side, as shown, and cut the fabric, adding a ½" seam allowance on all four sides. Repeat for the second piece of exterior fabric.

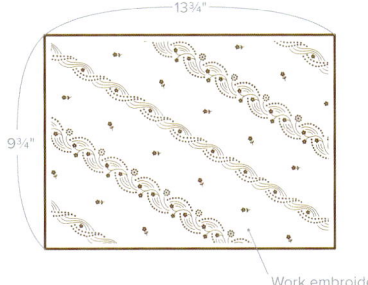

13¾"

9¾"

Work embroidery.

Assemble the two exterior fabrics, right sides together, and sew together, leaving an opening for turning out.

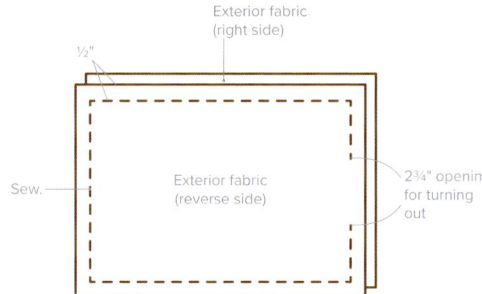

Exterior fabric (right side)

½"

Sew.

Exterior fabric (reverse side)

2¾" opening for turning out

Turn right side out, and lightly iron to reshape. Insert craft batting through the opening for turning out.

With a U-shaped ladder stitch, sew the opening closed. Make 4 tassels (see p. 87). Sew the tassels onto the four corners.

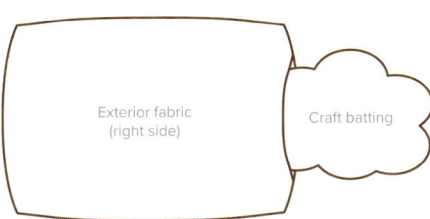

Exterior fabric (right side)

Craft batting

U-shaped ladder stitch

Sew on the tassels.

Townhouses

KEY CASE | page 31

Finished size: 2¾" x 4" (main area)

∗ DMC No. 25 embroidery floss: 310, 3866,
   1 skein each

Materials

Exterior fabric: Linen, camel/beige, 7⅞" x 9¾"

Lining fabric: Linen, unbleached, 6" x 9¾"

One-sided fusible quilt batting (soft, lightweight),
   6" x 7⅞"

⅛"-wide leather cord, 11¾", 1 piece

1¼"-diameter metal keyring, 1 piece

Machine-sewing thread, beige, as needed

How to Make

1

Transfer the embroidery pattern (full-size pattern insert, side A), onto the right side of the exterior fabric. Embroider the pattern (embroidery instructions on p. 70), and iron your work lightly. Trace the pattern edges onto the reverse side, and cut the fabric, adding a ½" seam allowance all around. Repeat for the second piece of exterior fabric. Cut two pieces for the lining fabric in the same way.

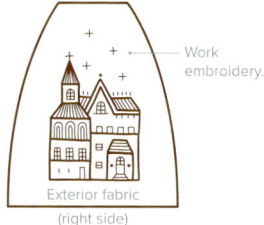

Work embroidery.

Exterior fabric
(right side)

2

Cut two pieces of the one-sided fusible quilt batting to the pattern dimensions. Place the fusible side of one piece of quilt batting on the reverse side of the embroidered work, and if you're using a pressing cloth, lay that on top before using an iron to activate the adhesive. Repeat with second piece of quilt batting on second piece of exterior fabric.

*Do not attach the quilt batting to the lining fabric.

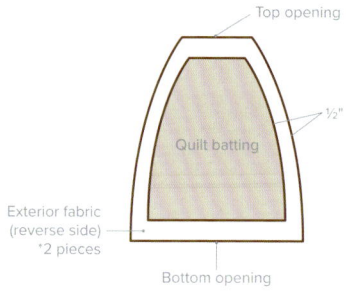

Top opening

Quilt batting

½"

Exterior fabric
(reverse side)
*2 pieces

Bottom opening

3

When the fabrics from step 2 are cool and the quilt batting has fully adhered, assemble the two exterior fabrics, right sides together, and sew together on both sides. Repeat with the lining fabric. Trim the seam allowances to ¼" and make cuts along the curves.

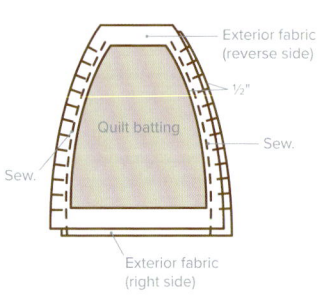

Exterior fabric
(reverse side)

½"

Quilt batting

Sew.

Sew.

Exterior fabric
(right side)

4

Open the seam allowances at the top openings of the exterior fabric and the lining fabric and assemble them, right sides together, then sew these together.

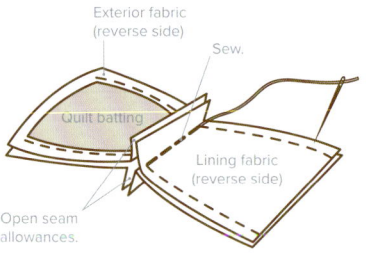

Exterior fabric
(reverse side)

Sew.

Quilt batting

Lining fabric
(reverse side)

Open seam
allowances.

5

Turn right side out through the bottom opening and reshape. Fold the seam allowances on the bottom edges of the exterior fabric and the lining fabric toward the inside and use whipstitches to close these together.

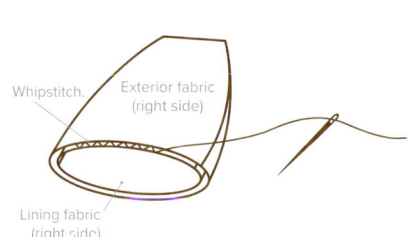

Whipstitch.

Exterior fabric
(right side)

Lining fabric
(right side)

6

Fold the leather cord in half and loop the folded end around the keyring. Pass the cord through the case from the bottom and tie a square knot at the end of the cord.

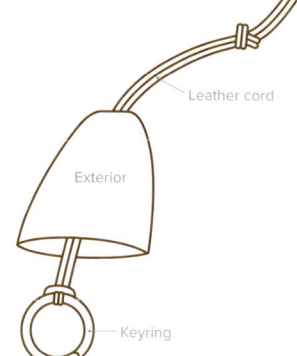

Leather cord

Exterior

Keyring

Roadside

BOOK COVER AND BOOKMARK | page 33

BOOK COVER

Finished size: 16½" x 9"

* DMC No. 25 embroidery floss: 823, 840, 918, 3866, 1 skein each

Materials

Exterior fabric: Linen, unbleached, 22" x 12"

Lining fabric: Linen, white, 22" x 12"

½"-wide ribbon, unbleached, 10½", 1 piece

Machine-sewing thread, unbleached, as needed

BOOKMARK

Finished size: 2⅜" x 4¼"

* DMC No. 25 embroidery floss: 3866, 1 skein

Materials

Exterior fabric: Linen, navy blue, 6" x 7⅞", 2 pieces

Double-sided fusible interfacing, 4" x 6"

¼"-wide ribbon, red, 4", 1 piece

Machine-sewing thread, navy blue, as needed

Finishing stitches: No. 25 embroidery floss DMC 823, 1 skein

How to Make the Book Cover

Transfer the embroidery pattern (p. 71) onto the right side of the exterior fabric. Embroider the pattern, and iron your work lightly. Trace the finished dimensions onto the reverse side, as shown, and cut the fabric, adding a ½" seam allowance all around. Cut the lining fabric in the same way.

Assemble the exterior fabric and lining fabric, right sides together, and sew the edges together on the pocket flap side.

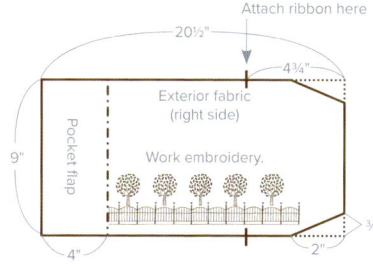

Attach ribbon here
20½"
4¾"
Exterior fabric (right side)
9"
Pocket flap
Work embroidery.
½"
4"
¾"
2"

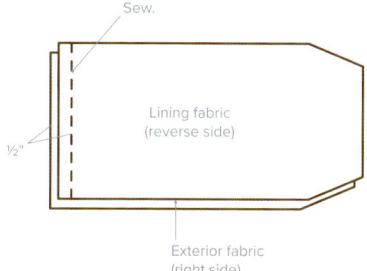

Sew.
Lining fabric (reverse side)
½"
Exterior fabric (right side)

Fold the pocket flap inward, as shown, and place the ribbon in between the fabrics at the attachment mark. Except for the pocket-flap side, sew together all around, leaving an opening for turning out. Trim the seam allowances to ¼" and make cuts at the corners.

Turn right side out, and lightly iron to reshape. With a U-shaped ladder stitch, sew the opening closed.

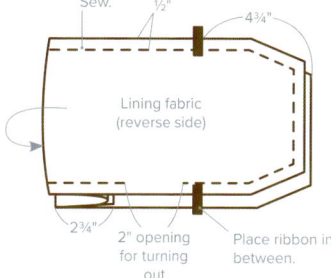

Sew.
½"
4¾"
Lining fabric (reverse side)
2¾"
2" opening for turning out
Place ribbon in between.

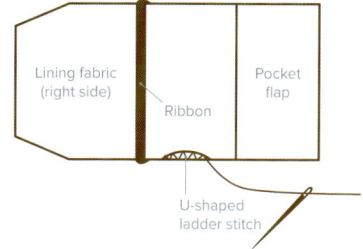

Lining fabric (right side)
Ribbon
Pocket flap
U-shaped ladder stitch

How to Make the Bookmark

Transfer the embroidery pattern (p. 71) onto the right side of the exterior fabric. Embroider the pattern, and iron your work lightly. Trace the pattern edges onto the reverse side, and cut the fabric, adding a ¼" seam allowance on all four sides. Repeat for the second piece of exterior fabric, and cut the double-sided fusible interfacing in the same way.

Assemble the exterior fabrics with the double-sided fusible interfacing in between, and insert the ribbon, folded in half, at the attachment mark. If you're using a pressing cloth, lay that on top before using an iron to activate the adhesive.

Sew the finishing stitches using thread in the same color as the fabric.

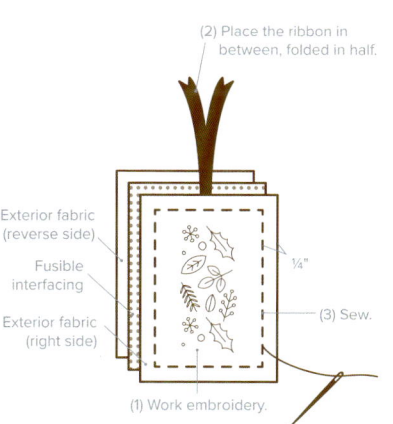

(2) Place the ribbon in between, folded in half.
Exterior fabric (reverse side)
Fusible interfacing
Exterior fabric (right side)
¼"
(3) Sew.
(1) Work embroidery.

Botanical Crown

CROWN | page 35

Finished size: 16½" x 3½" (main area)

* DMC No. 25 embroidery floss: 739, 833, 869, 895, 3346, 1 skein each

Materials

Exterior fabric: Linen, unbleached, 19¾" x 7⅞", 2 pieces

1½"-wide linen ribbon, unbleached, 19¾", 2 pieces

Machine-sewing thread, unbleached, as needed

How to Make

Transfer the embroidery pattern (p. 72) onto the right side of one of the exterior fabric pieces. Embroider the pattern, and iron your work lightly. Trace the pattern edges onto the reverse side, and cut the fabric, adding a ½" seam allowance all around. Repeat for the second piece of exterior fabric.

Assemble the two exterior fabrics, right sides together as shown, and place the ribbons in between the fabrics on either side. Sew together all around, leaving an opening for turning out. Trim the seam allowances to ¼" and make cuts at the corners.

Turn right side out, and lightly iron to reshape. With a U-shaped ladder stitch, sew the opening closed.

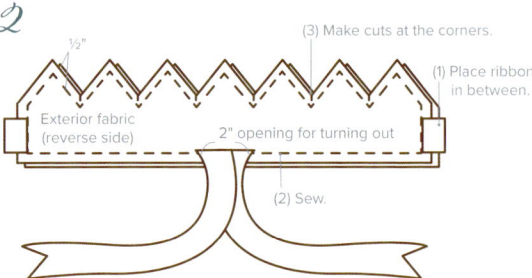

Exterior fabric (right side) — Work embroidery.

2⅜"

1⅜"

2¼"

3⅝"

16⅝"

½"

(3) Make cuts at the corners.

(1) Place ribbon in between.

Exterior fabric (reverse side)

2" opening for turning out

(2) Sew.

Festive Flowers

DETACHED COLLAR | page 37

Finished size: Neckline 14½"

* DMC No. 25 embroidery floss: 522, 600, 834, 904, 962, 986, 3755, 3847, 3865, 1 skein each

Materials

Exterior fabric: Linen, white, 15¾" x 7⅞", 2 pieces

½"-wide linen ribbon, white, 11¾", 2 pieces

Machine-sewing thread, white, as needed

How to Make

Transfer the embroidery pattern (full-size pattern insert, side A) onto the right side of one of the exterior fabric pieces. Embroider the pattern (embroidery instructions on p. 73), and iron your work lightly. Trace the pattern edges onto the reverse side, and cut the fabric, adding a ½" seam allowance all around. Repeat for the second piece of exterior fabric.

Assemble the two exterior fabrics, right sides together, and place the ribbons in between the fabrics on either side, as shown. Sew together all around, leaving an opening for turning out. Make cuts along the curves.

Turn right side out, and lightly iron to reshape. With a U-shaped ladder stitch, sew the opening closed.

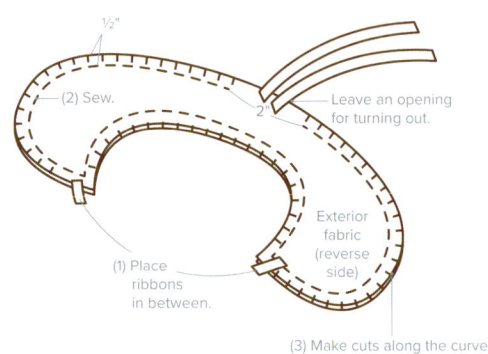

½"

(2) Sew.

Leave an opening for turning out.

2"

Exterior fabric (reverse side)

(1) Place ribbons in between.

(3) Make cuts along the curve.

Eden

SHOULDER BAG | page 39

Finished size: 13¾" x 10½" (excluding shoulder strap)

* DMC No. 25 embroidery floss: 3033, 3 skeins

Materials

Exterior fabric: Linen, pink, 15¾" x 24"

Lining fabric: Linen, unbleached, 15¾" x 24"

Shoulder strap fabric: Linen, pink, 17¾" x 4"

Ribbon fabric: Linen, pink, 13¾" x 1½", 2 pieces

Machine-sewing thread, pink, as needed

How to Make

1

Using an iron, press folds into the fabric for the shoulder strap as shown and machine stitch both edges. Press folds in the ribbon fabric in the same way, and machine stitch along one edge. Make 2 ribbons.

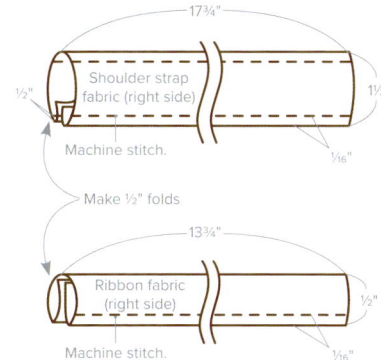

2

Transfer the embroidery pattern (p. 74) onto the right side of the exterior fabric. Embroider the pattern, and iron your work lightly. Trace the finished dimensions onto the reverse side, as shown, and cut the fabric, adding a ½" seam allowance on all four sides. Cut the lining fabric in the same way.

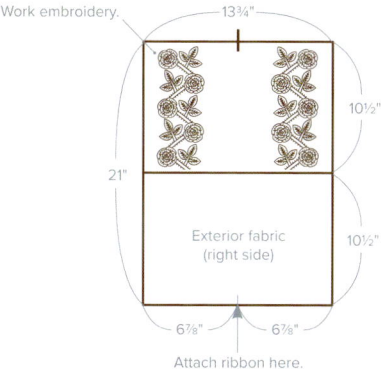

3

Fold the exterior fabric in half, right sides together, and sew together on both sides. Press seam allowances open. Sew the lining fabric together in the same way, leaving an opening for turning out.

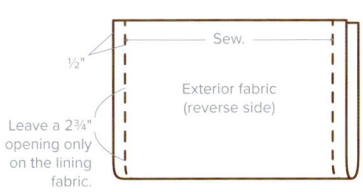

4

Assemble the exterior bag and interior bag, right sides together. In between the exterior and interior bags, insert the shoulder strap on each side and the ribbons from step 1 at the attachment marks in the center, as shown, and sew around the mouth of the bag. *You can reinforce where the shoulder strap is attached by backstitching several times.

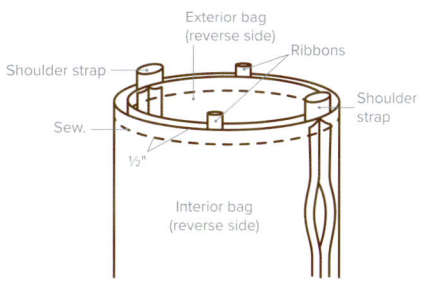

5

Turn right side out, and lightly iron to reshape. With a U-shaped ladder stitch, sew the opening closed.

Floral Scale Pattern

DRAWSTRING PURSE | page 41

Finished size: 9¼" x 12½"

* DMC No. 25 embroidery floss: 28, 223, 224, 500, 647, 3721, 3866, 1 skein each

Materials

Exterior fabric: Linen, white, 11¾" x 27½"
Lining fabric: Linen, pale gray, 11¾" x 24"
Casing fabric: Linen, white, 9¾" x 6"
½"-wide string, white, 19¾", 2 pieces
Machine-sewing thread, white, as needed

How to Make

1

Cut the fabric for the casings, adding a ½" seam allowance on all four sides. On the short ends, fold the seam allowances. Machine stitch, and fold the piece in half again lengthwise.

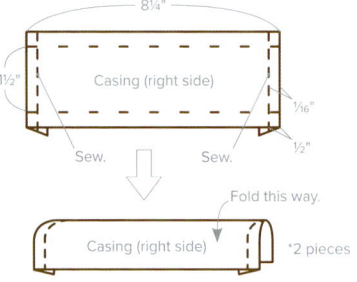

2

Transfer the embroidery pattern (full-size pattern insert, side B) onto the right side of one of the exterior fabric pieces. Embroider the pattern (embroidery instructions on p. 75), and iron your work lightly. Trace the pattern edges onto the reverse side, and cut the fabric, adding a ½" seam allowance all around. Cut another exterior piece of fabric.

3

Trace the dimensions for the lining fabric on the reverse side, as shown, and cut out, adding a ½" seam allowance on all four sides. Fold the lining fabric in half, right sides together, and sew together on both sides, leaving an opening for turning out.

4

Assemble the exterior fabrics, right sides together, and sew around the edges, leaving the mouth open. Make cuts along the seam allowances of the curves.

5

Assemble the exterior bag and interior bag from step 3, right sides together, then insert the casings from step 1 on either side, with the folds facing downward, in between the exterior and interior bags. Sew around the mouth of the bag.

6

Turn right side out, and lightly iron to reshape. With a U-shaped ladder stitch, sew the opening closed. Insert the strings through both sides of the casings and tie the ends.

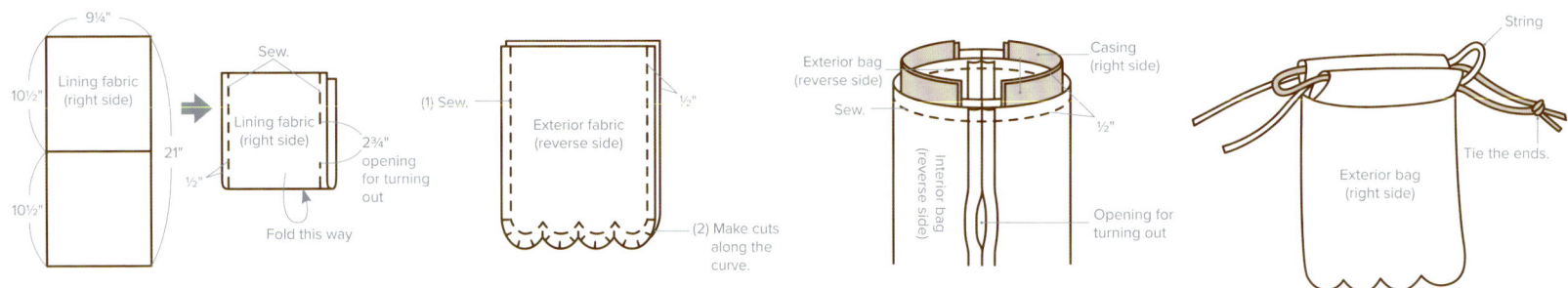

Four Seasons of Flowers

CLOTH BOX | page 43

Finished size: 1¾" H x 3½" L x 3½" W

* DMC No. 25 embroidery floss: 501, 502, 554, 739, 832, 931, 3755, 3866, 1 skein each

Materials

Exterior fabric for lid: Linen, dark green, 11¾" x 11¾"

Lining fabric for lid: Linen, green, 9¾" x 9¾"

Exterior fabric for base: Linen, dark green, 11¾" x 11¾"

Lining fabric for base: Linen, green, 9¾" x 9¾"

One-sided fusible quilt batting (soft, lightweight), 7⅞" x 15¾"

Machine-sewing thread, green, as needed

How to Make

Transfer the embroidery pattern (full-size pattern insert, side B) onto the right side of the exterior fabric for the lid. Embroider the pattern (embroidery instructions on p. 73), and iron your work lightly. Trace the pattern edges onto the reverse side, and cut the fabric, adding a ½" seam allowance all around. Cut the lining fabric for the lid in the same way.

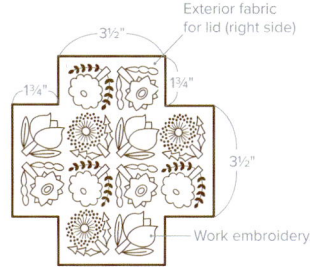

Exterior fabric for lid (right side)

3½" · 1¾" · 1¾" · 3½"

Work embroidery.

Trace the dimensions for the exterior fabric for the base on the reverse side, as shown, and cut out, adding a ½" seam allowance all around. Cut the lining fabric for the base in the same way.

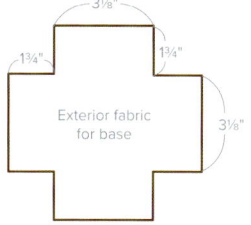

3⅛" · 1¾" · 1¾" · 3⅛"

Exterior fabric for base

Cut the quilt batting to the dimensions of each of the fabrics from steps 1 and 2. Place the fusible side of the quilt batting on the reverse side of the embroidered work for the exterior fabric for the lid, and on the reverse side of the exterior fabric for the base, and if you're using a pressing cloth, lay that on top before using an iron to activate the adhesive.
*Do not attach the quilt batting to the lining fabric.

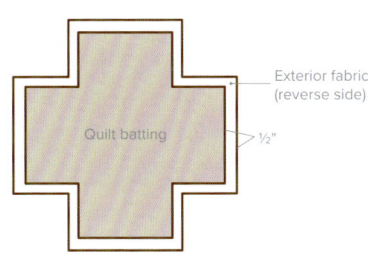

Quilt batting

Exterior fabric (reverse side)

½"

When the fabric from step 3 is cool and the quilt batting has fully adhered, sew the adjoining sides together by folding the exterior fabric in half, right sides together, to form the shape of a box. Sew the lining fabric together in the same way. Do this for both the lid and the base.

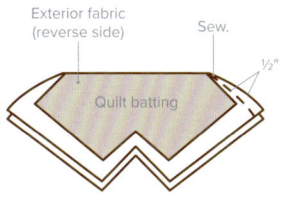

Exterior fabric (reverse side)

Sew.

½"

Quilt batting

Assemble the exterior fabric and interior fabric, right sides together, and sew the top edges together, leaving an opening for turning out. Do this for both the lid and the base.

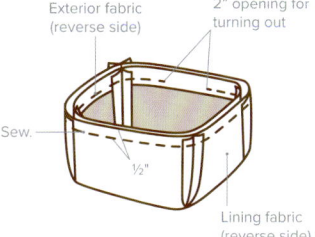

Exterior fabric (reverse side)

2" opening for turning out

Sew.

½"

Lining fabric (reverse side)

Turn right side out, and lightly iron to reshape. With a U-shaped ladder stitch, sew the opening closed.

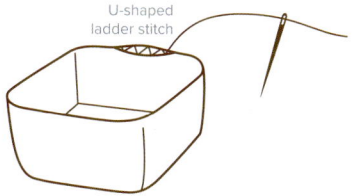

U-shaped ladder stitch

Ivy

BRACELET | page 45

Finished size: 6¾" x 2¼"
* DMC No. 25 embroidery floss: 610, 1 skein

Materials

Exterior fabric: Linen, black, 9¾" x 6", 2 pieces
One-sided fusible quilt batting (soft, lightweight),
    6¾" x 2¼"
¼"-wide cord, black, 2⅜", 1 piece
⅝"-diameter button, 1 piece
Machine-sewing thread, black, as needed

How to Make

Transfer the embroidery pattern (p. 76) onto the right side of
one piece of the exterior fabric. Embroider the pattern, and iron
your work lightly. Trace the pattern edges onto the reverse side,
and cut the fabric, adding a ½" seam allowance on all four sides.
Repeat for the second piece of exterior fabric.

Exterior fabric
(right side)

6¾"

2¼"

Attach
cord here.

Work embroidery.

Assemble with the other piece of exterior fabric, right sides
together. Fold the cord in half and insert it, with the fold toward
the inside, in between the fabrics at the attachment mark, and sew
together, leaving an opening for turning out. Place the fusible side
of the quilt batting on the reverse side of the embroidered work,
and if you're using a pressing cloth, lay that on top before using an
iron to activate the adhesive.

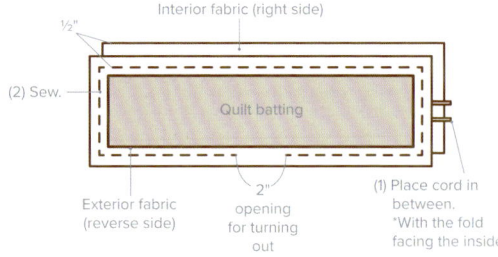

Interior fabric (right side)

½"

(2) Sew.

Quilt batting

Exterior fabric
(reverse side)

2"
opening
for turning
out

(1) Place cord in
between.
*With the fold
facing the inside

When the fabric from step 2 is cool and the quilt batting has fully
adhered, trim the seam allowances to ¼" and turn right side out.
Lightly iron again to reshape, and sew the opening closed with a
U-shaped ladder stitch.

Sew the button onto the exterior fabric.

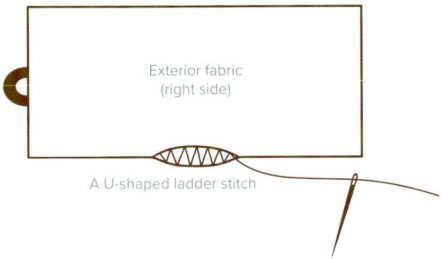

Exterior fabric
(right side)

A U-shaped ladder stitch

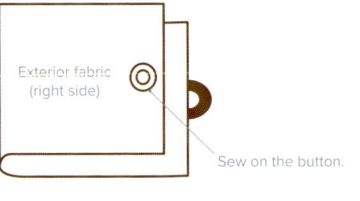

Exterior fabric
(right side)

Sew on the button.

The Trees

MOUNTAIN-SHAPED TEA COZY | page 47

Finished size: 12¼" x 8¼"

＊ DMC No. 25 embroidery floss: 3024, 3 skeins

Materials

Exterior fabric: Linen, dark green, 15¾" x 24"

Lining: Quilt cloth, 15¾" x 24"

Loop fabric: Linen, dark green, 4" x 1½"

Machine-sewing thread, dark green, as needed

How to Make

Using an iron, press folds into the fabric for the loop, as shown, and machine stitch the edge.

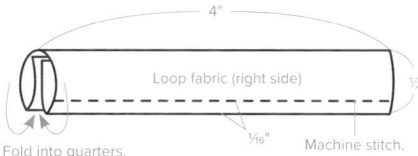

4"

Loop fabric (right side)   ½"

Fold into quarters.   ¹⁄₁₆"   Machine stitch.

Transfer the embroidery pattern (full-size pattern insert, side B) onto the right side of one of the exterior fabric pieces. Embroider the pattern (embroidery instructions on p. 77), and iron your work lightly. Trace the pattern edges onto the reverse side, and cut the fabric, adding a ½" seam allowance all around. Cut another exterior piece of fabric.

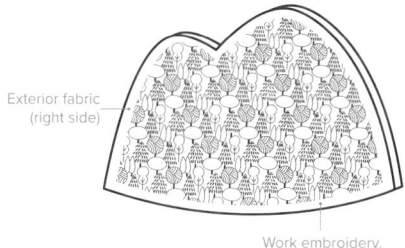

Exterior fabric (right side)

Work embroidery.

Assemble the exterior fabric from step 2 with right sides together. Fold and insert the loop from step 1 in between these at the attachment mark, with the fold toward the inside, and sew together, leaving an opening at the bottom. Trim the seam allowances to a ¼" and make cuts along the curves. Sew the lining fabric together in the same way, leaving an opening for turning out.
*Please refer to step 3 on page 80 for instructions on lining with quilt cloth.

Insert the exterior fabric inside the lining fabric from step 3, right sides together, and sew together along the bottom edge.
*For the quilt cloth lining, instead of making cuts along the curve, trim the seam allowance to ¹⁄₁₆".

Turn right side out, and lightly iron to reshape. With a U-shaped ladder stitch, sew the opening closed.

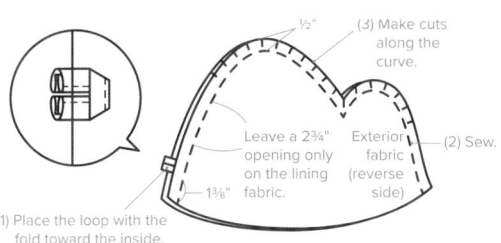

½"   (3) Make cuts along the curve.

Leave a 2¾" opening only on the lining fabric.

Exterior fabric (reverse side)

(2) Sew.

(1) Place the loop with the fold toward the inside.

1⅜"

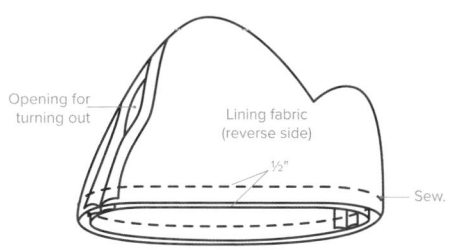

Opening for turning out

Lining fabric (reverse side)

½"

Sew.

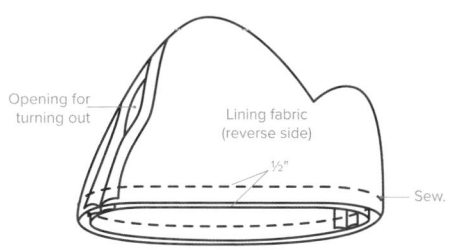

Chickens and Eggs

MINI BASKET | page 49

Finished size: 4" diameter x 2" H

* DMC No. 25 embroidery floss: 310, 520, 646, 733, 919, 3865, 1 skein each

Materials

Exterior fabric: Linen, gray, 19¾" x 7⅞"

Lining: Linen, gray, 19¾" x 7⅞"

Handle fabric: Linen, gray, 4¾" x 1½", 2 pieces

One-sided fusible quilt batting (soft, lightweight), 15¾" x 7⅞"

Machine-sewing thread, gray, as needed

How to Make

Using an iron, press folds into the fabric for the handle as shown and machine stitch along one edge. Make 2 handles.

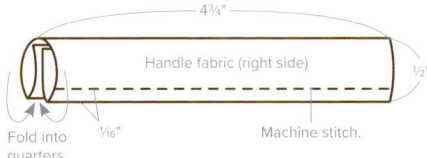

Transfer the embroidery pattern (full-size pattern insert, side B) onto the right side of the exterior fabric. Embroider the pattern (embroidery instructions on p. 78), and iron your work lightly. Trace the pattern edges onto the reverse side, and cut the fabric, adding a ½" seam allowance on all four sides. Cut the lining fabric in the same way. Cut exterior fabric and lining fabric for the basket bottom as well.

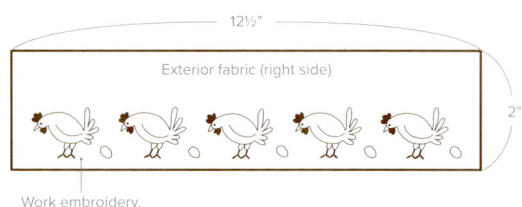

Cut the one-sided fusible quilt batting to the dimensions shown below. Place the fusible side of the quilt batting on the reverse side of the embroidered work, and if you're using a pressing cloth, lay that on top before using an iron to activate the adhesive. Adhere the quilt batting to the exterior fabric for the basket bottom in the same way.
*Do not attach the quilt batting to the lining fabric.

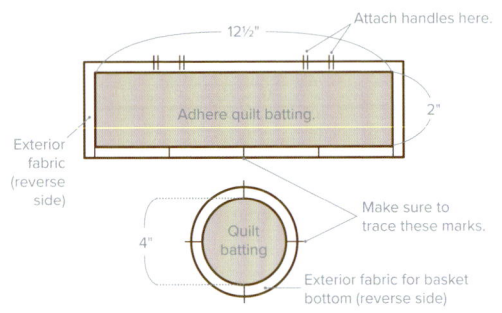

When the fabric from step 3 is cool and the quilt batting has fully adhered, fold the exterior fabric in half, right sides together, and sew the edges together. Sew the lining fabric together in the same way.

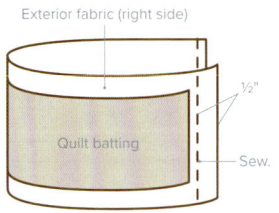

Assemble the exterior fabric from step 4 and the basket bottom from step 3, right sides together, and use closely spaced whipstitches to sew these together. Trim the seam allowance to ¼" and make cuts along the curve. Sew the lining fabric together in the same way.
*Use basting stitches when sewing the basket bottom to keep it in place.

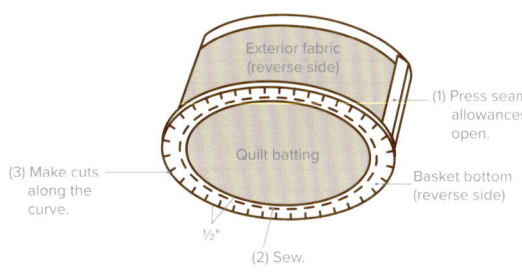

6

Assemble the exterior bag and interior bag, right sides together. Fold the handles in half and insert them at the attachment marks on each side, in between the exterior and interior bags. Sew together around the upper edge, leaving an opening for turning out.

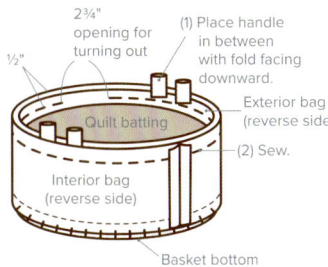

7

Turn right side out, and lightly iron to reshape. With a U-shaped ladder stitch, sew the opening closed.

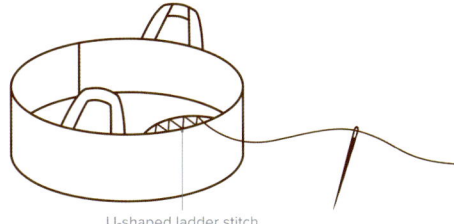

U-shaped ladder stitch

Flower Row

CENTERPIECE TABLE RUNNER | page 4

Finished size: 23" x 6"

* DMC No. 25 embroidery floss: 3777, about 3 skeins

Materials

Exterior fabric: Linen, unbleached, 25¾" x 7⅞", 2 pieces

Machine-sewing thread, unbleached, as needed

How to Make

1

Transfer the embroidery pattern (full-size pattern insert, side B) onto the right side of one of the exterior fabric pieces. Embroider the pattern, and iron your work lightly. Trace the dimensions, as shown, onto the reverse side, and cut the fabric, adding a ½" seam allowance on all four sides. Cut another exterior piece of fabric in the same way.

2

Assemble the two exterior fabrics, right sides together, and sew together, leaving a 2¾" opening for turning out.

3

Turn right side out, and lightly iron to reshape. With a U-shaped ladder stitch, sew the opening closed.

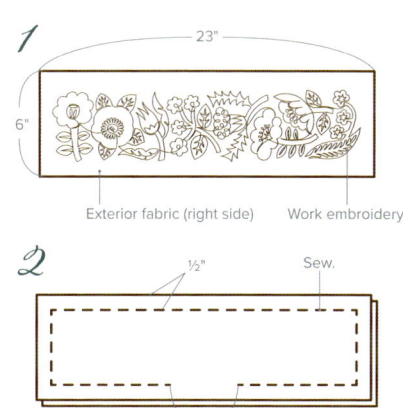

1

23"

6"

Exterior fabric (right side)   Work embroidery.

2

½"

Sew.

2¾" opening for turning out

Yumiko Higuchi

After graduating from Tama Art University, Yumiko Higuchi worked as a handbag designer. Her pieces were shown and sold in boutiques. She began creating embroidery designs in 2008. She produces original embroidery patterns that feature botanical motifs and all manner of insects and living creatures.

Roost Books

An imprint of Shambhala Publications, Inc.
2129 13th Street
Boulder, Colorado 80302
www.shambhala.com

Translation © 2024 by Shambhala Publications, Inc.
Translation by Allison Markin Powell
Originally published as *Higuchi Yumiko tsunagaru shishu* © 2021 by Yumiko Higuchi
Educational Foundation Bunka Gakuen, Bunka Publishing Bureau
English translation rights arranged with Educational Foundation Bunka Gakuen, Bunka Publishing Bureau through Japan UNI Agency, Inc., Tokyo

Bunka Publishing Bureau Staff Credits

Publisher: Katsuhiro Hamada
Book Design: Hiroaki Seki (Mr. Universe)
Photography: Akiko Arai
Styling: Kaori Maeda
Hair and Makeup: KOMAKI (nomadica)
Models: Cailyn Nelson, Sofia Gheorghiu (Sugar & Spice)
DTP: Yoshie Fujishiro
Proofreader: Masako Mukai
Editors: Mariko Tsuchiya (Three Season); Kaori Tanaka (Bunka Publishing Bureau)

Parts of this book appeared in a series featured in *Misesu* magazine, from January to December 2017, forming the basis for these contents, which have been updated and expanded.

9 8 7 6 5 4 3 2

Printed in China

Shambhala Publications makes every effort to print on acid-free, recycled paper. Shambhala Publications is distributed worldwide by Penguin Random House, Inc., and its subsidiaries.

Library of Congress Cataloging-in-Publication Data

Names: Higuchi, Yumiko, 1975– author. | Powell, Allison Markin, translator.
Title: Seamless embroidery: 42 projects and patterns to explore the magic of repeating designs / Yumiko Higuchi; translation by Allison Markin Powell.
Other titles: Higuchi Yumiko tsunagaru shishu. English
Description: Boulder, Colorado: Roost Books, an imprint of Shambhala Publications, Inc., [2024] | Translation of: Higuchi Yumiko tsunagaru shishu, 2021.
Identifiers: LCCN 2023029409 | ISBN 9781645471929 (trade paperback)
Subjects: LCSH: Embroidery—Japan—Patterns.
Classification: LCC TT769.J3 H53913 2024 | DDC 746.440280952—dc23/eng/20230724
LC record available at https://lccn.loc.gov/2023029409

The authorized representative in the EU for product safety and compliance is eucomply OÜ, Pärnu mnt 139b-14, 11317 Tallinn, Estonia, hello@eucompliancepartner.com.